Alvar Aalto Houses

Alvar Aalto Houses

Jari Jetsonen and Sirkkaliisa Jetsonen

with an introduction by Juhani Pallasmaa

Princeton Architectural Press · New York

Contents

previous, page 2: **Villa Skeppet (Villa Schildt),**
view of the living room, Tammisaari,
Finland, 1969–70

Acknowledgments

We are grateful to all those whose generous contributions have made this book possible. Especially, we would like to thank the author of the introductory essay, architect and professor Juhani Pallasmaa, for his thoughtful and sensitive contribution enriching this book. Special thanks go to editor Nicola Bednarek Brower of Princeton Architectural Press for having faith in this project.

The greatest thanks, however, go to the owners of the houses and their relatives who allowed us into their private homes to photograph them and assisted us in finding archival material relating to the buildings: Usko Paananen, Jyväskylä; Lauri Laapotti, Laukkavirta; Rauni Aho, Töysä; Eeva-Marjatta Karstu, Jyväskylä; Paavo Tammekann, Vantaa; Heikki Alanen, Helsinki; Päivi Tötterman, Kotka; Tiia Kivinen, Inkeroinen; Hanna Myllyntausta, Inkeroinen; Kristian Gullichsen, Helsinki; Pennefors & Häggblom, Tampere; Veikko Niemi, Mikkeli; Jarno Kattelus, Hämeenlinna; Marjaleena and Jaakko Lahti, Pori: Johanna Söderholm, Helsinki; Helena and Noora Langinvainio, Helsinki; Markku Lahti, Jyväskylä; Markku Huotari family, Oulu; Ásdís Ólafsdóttir, Paris; Arja and Erkki Hämäläinen, Hamina; Marjaliisa Uski, Hamina; Erika and Rauno Karhu, Hamina; Ari Aho, Helsinki; Else and Pellervo Oksala, Helsinki; Joonas and Anita Kokkonen, Järvenpää; and Christine and Göran Schildt, Tammisaari.

We wish to thank the Alvar Aalto Foundation for all its help, especially the curators at the Alvar Aalto Museum, Katariina Pakoma, Marja Holma, and Risto Raittila; and the curators at the Alvar Aalto Foundation, Mia Hipeli and Arne Hästesko, who have generously provided help finding written documents, drawings, and photographs in their archives. Executive director Jennifer Dahlbäck at the Christine and Göran Schildt Foundation has provided helpful information on the Villa Skeppet. Architect Nicholas Mayow translated the foreword and edited parts of the text of the main chapters.

We would also like to thank and remember the late Erkki Luoma, who used to work as an architect in Alvar Aalto's office (1954–68). We met him some thirty years ago on the terrace of the restaurant Elite in Helsinki, and he graciously told us about the daily routine in the Aalto office, of his time spent at the Muuratsalo Experimental House working on architectural competitions, and his trip with Aalto to the CIAM conference in France in 1953, where they met Le Corbusier and other legendary architects of the modern movement. At the end of our conversation, he presented us with a Czechoslovakian mechanical pencil that Aalto had once given to him. Afterwards we indeed noticed a similar pencil in the maestro's hand in archival photographs. We can say that the pencil has served us well while writing this book.

Sirkkaliisa and Jari Jetsonen
Helsinki, February 3, 2010

Foreword

When entering our old churches, gazing at a Gustavian (Scandinavian rococo) country manor or examining a century-old work of rural handicraft, we are seized by emotion. No doubt this is partly due to the trace of human handwork on the surface, the artistic purity of building materials or the simple lines adapted to our landscape; on the other hand, it also has to do with the signs of wear and centuries of patina in the building material.
—Alvar Aalto, "Motifs from Past Ages," 1922

When we enter an Alvar Aalto building or house today, in the early years of the twenty-first century, we encounter the very same characteristics: human craft, artistic purity in the use of materials, and a design that merges with its surroundings. There is also a beautiful patina expressing the life span of his houses.

When talking and writing about architecture, Aalto often referred to nature and biology. "Architecture must be modeled after the biological forms of nature," was one of his oft-used slogans. According to the architect, buildings are born, they learn what real life is like, and it is only after twenty years that we can judge their quality. Ecological solutions such as the choice of natural materials and a respect for nature were basic values of Aalto's throughout his career.

During the late 1920s his architecture underwent a period of transition from classicism to the International Style and functionalism. The architect was enthusiastically interested in new ideas and rational design methods. The Paimio Tuberculosis Sanatorium (1929–33), which is regarded as a masterpiece of the so-called heroic functionalism, made him world-famous in a short period of time. Several private houses by Aalto, for example the Villa Tammekann (1932–33), also reflect the strict design principles of the Bauhaus, but Aalto never lost the basis he had adopted. Vernacular architecture and building methods were always present in his work, whether we look at luxurious houses such as the Villa Mairea (1938–39) and the Maison Carré (1956–59) or the log saunas he designed for himself and several clients as late as the late 1960s. In Aalto's functionalism we can detect a romantic quality, a kind of "hidden presence" of the past, as architectural historian William J. R. Curtis put it.

Looking at Aalto's houses enables us to observe the changes—or development—his architecture underwent from the early 1920s until the 1970s.

It is a chain of almost one hundred projects of which more than half were never realized. His great villas, including the unrealized Villa Sambonet (1955) and Villa Erica (1970), were case studies. Here he had the opportunity to experiment and study architectural and technical solutions that could later be used in ordinary homes.

On the other hand, Aalto also studied and designed prefabricated houses from the 1920s onwards. Social consciousness and optimism were an important part of his work, especially during the war and postwar years. He was a reformer who wanted to improve the life of the common man. His idea was to build "paradises for ordinary people" and give life a gentler structure. In this book, texts by experts Juhani Pallasmaa and Sirkkaliisa Jetsonen, with excellent photos by Jari Jetsonen, illustrate how Alvar Aalto realized these dreams.

Markku Lahti
Director of the Alvar Aalto Foundation

Alvar Aalto's Concept of Dwelling

Juhani Pallasmaa

The setting of Alvar Aalto's birth and earliest childhood. His father, surveyor J. H. Aalto, rented the upper story of this farmhouse in Kuortane, Finland, where Alvar was born on February 3, 1898. His family moved to Jyväskylä, a small town in central Finland, in 1903, when Alvar was five years old.

opposite
Aalto in front of the living room fireplace at the Muuratsalo Experimental House in the 1950s

The most basic and, at the same time, arguably the most demanding architectural task is the design of the individual dwelling. The deepest architectural emotions, images, and associations are concretized in this most intimate of design tasks. Only structures built for the purposes of faith pose similarly subtle existential, emotive, and personal issues.

During his exceptionally productive career that lasted more than half a century and extended from planning and architecture to product design and artistic work, Alvar Aalto designed numerous dwellings, from one-family houses and weekend residences to apartment buildings and entire housing areas for municipalities and industrial companies. His clients ranged from privileged and wealthy patrons; to his friends, such as his biographer Göran Schildt, his favorite architectural photographer Eino Mäkinen, and taxi driver Alvi Hirvonen; to the anonymous dwellers of apartment blocks. The catalog of Aalto's oeuvre compiled by Schildt lists seventy-six projects for houses and vacation dwellings; forty-five terraced houses, apartment buildings, and housing areas; and thirty-eight projects for standardized housing.[1] He also designed and built a house and two summer residences for his own family, in addition to working on the family's apartments, which he altered and furnished earlier in his career. Aalto's standardized housing systems include designs for reconstruction projects after World War Two. Even his research at the Massachusetts Institute of Technology in 1940 dealt with prefabricated housing adapted to differing site conditions and family structures.

The architect also frequently wrote and spoke about technical, psychological, and social problems related to dwelling and housing. One of his earliest essays, entitled "From Doorstep to Living Room," written at the age of twenty-eight in 1926, is his most important literary study of dwelling.[2] It reveals that he approached the issue of dwelling and home from a mental and experiential point of view rather than from the aspect of utility or an aestheticized architectural formalism. In this essay, we find the foundations for many of the design elements that characterized Aalto's early classicist houses as well as his later modernist designs.

The essence of the article is to point out ways in which the long traditions of dwelling in the south, which have developed through millennia of life and architectural history, could be transferred to the Nordic climatic and cultural conditions. The architect admired Mediterranean culture to the degree that at the

Fra Angelico's painting *Annunciation* (ca. 1432–33) illustrates one of the central themes of Aalto's essay "From Doorstep to Living Room": Aalto's ideal image of homecoming.

Niemelä farmhouse, Konginkangas, Seurasaari Open-Air Museum. A traditional Finnish farmhouse with a loosely enclosed courtyard in the vicinity of the Aalto House in Helsinki, which Aalto greatly admired as a model for dwelling.

Le Corbusier, Pavillon de l'Esprit Nouveau, Paris, 1925. Aalto's illustration is slightly cropped on all four sides, and the traditional light fitting on the balustrade and the building behind the tree have been retouched.

time of writing his essay, he entertained ambitions to turn his humble hometown in central Finland, Jyväskylä, into "the Florence of the North."[3]

One of the images with which Aalto illustrated his essay is Fra Angelico's painting *Annunciation* (ca. 1432–33), the subtle architecture of which reflects the ideals of Nordic classicism in the 1920s, which was inspired by the *architettura minore* of northern Italy. As Aalto writes:

> We find in its miniature form a great deal of truth and refinement to illustrate our problem. The picture provides an ideal example of "entering a room." The trinity of *human being, room and garden* [Aalto's italics] shown in the picture makes it an unattainable ideal image of the home. The same smile which plays on the face of the Holy Virgin is seen in the delicate details of the building and in the brilliant flowers in the garden. Two things stand out plainly: the unity of the room, the external wall and the garden, and the formation of these elements so as to give the human figure prominence and express her state of mind.[4]

The articulation of the interplay of landscape and architecture, nature and artifice, outside and inside, would become a constant theme in Aalto's designs, from houses to public buildings. Although he points out the special limitations of designing in the Nordic context, Aalto develops ideas how to create this essential experiential unity of the various aspects of dwelling even in a cold climate:

> There is nothing wrong with our homes being closed to the outside world—so are those in the South, though for different reasons—but the screening element of our houses is almost invariably placed badly. The right spot for our doorstep is where we step out of the street or road into the garden.... The garden (or courtyard) belongs to our home just as much as any of the rooms. Let the step from the kitchen garden to the rooms provide a much smaller contrast than the one from the road or street to the garden.[5]

In order to acknowledge the climatic reality,

> The Finnish home should have two faces. One is the aesthetically direct contact with the world outside; the other, its winter face, turns inward and is seen in the interior design, which emphasizes the warmth of our inner rooms....I see the garden and the interior decoration as a closely-knit organism.[6]

In Aalto's own designs, the idea of the two faces of the dwelling appears in the contrast of the frequently rugged and masculine exterior and the softer, lighter, and somewhat feminine interior spaces.

Although Aalto's illustrations of the essay include a photograph of the balcony garden of Le Corbusier's Pavillon de l'Esprit Nouveau of 1925, which he admired as an ideal example of the affinity of the interior and the garden, Aalto clearly distanced himself from Le Corbusier's idea of "the house as a machine for living in."[7]

For him, an important element in the psychological mechanisms of the dwelling was the central hall, which, in Aalto's words, "symbolizes the open air under the home roof," and which the architect compared to the atrium of Roman houses.[8] A photograph of a ruined peristyle of a Pompeian patrician's house illustrates the interplay of the reversed images of interior and exterior. The atrium,

Perspective drawing of the hall in the Casa Väinö Aalto, Alajärvi, 1925, an unexecuted project for Alvar's younger brother, Väinö Aalto. Alvar's obsession with the Mediterranean atrium is evident in the design of the small hall, which is open to the second floor.

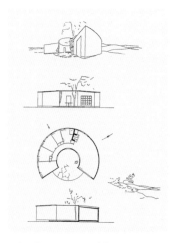

Aalto, "Merry-go-round," competition entry for vacation dwelling organized by the Finnish family journal *Aitta* in 1928

Aalto, apartment building, Hansaviertel, Berlin, 1955–57. View of the balcony-cum-courtyard on the left.

"at the same time forms the termination of the entrance area and the central space of the whole house. Its ceiling is the sky and the roofed rooms inside open up toward it."[9] Aalto demonstrated these ideas in his humble project for a Finnish house with a central miniaturized hall open to the second floor rather than the sky. The architect's later countless variations of skylights throughout his career are examples of his dialectics between interior space and the sky.

The courtyard, atrium, or enclosed balcony, also became a repeated theme in Aalto's designs for dwellings, from early competition entries for prefabricated vacation houses (1928 and 1932) to the Aalto House in Helsinki (1935), the Villa Mairea in Noormarkku (1938–39), the Experimental House in Muuratsalo (1952–53), Aalto's studio in Helsinki (1954–56), and the atrium-like balcony of his apartment building in the Hansaviertel of Berlin (1955–57).

At the end of his essay, Aalto interestingly introduces the theme of human weakness:

> Your home should purposely show up some weakness of yours. This may seem to be a field in which the architect's authority ceases, but no architectural creation is complete without some such trait; it will not be alive. This trait can be compared to the need for a particularly subtle kind of humour to expose one's own weaknesses.[10]

He would return to the theme of human weakness or error throughout his career. For the architect, weakness in the design of dwellings implies allowance for a deliberate tolerance, a margin for visual and stylistic deviation. He acknowledges that genuine and true homes are expressions of the dweller's personality rather than that of the architect's. The objects of home should be associated with the inhabitant's past, appreciations, and memories instead of being an aesthetic choice by the designer. Here Aalto seems to echo John Ruskin's ideas of the psychological value of incompleteness and imperfection:

> Imperfection is in some sort essential to all that we know of life. It is the sign of life in a mortal body, that is to say, of a process and change. Nothing that lives is, or can be rigidly perfect: part of it is decaying, part nascent.... And in all things that live there are certain inequalities and deficiencies, which are not only signs of life but sources of beauty.[11]

Many homes of the modern era can be experienced as too controlling and aesthetically predetermined to permit the inhabitant's personal adaptation and lifestyle. After all, there is a distinct contradiction, conflict, and tension between the concepts of "architecture" and "home." Whereas architecture is a product of deliberate design and aesthetic aspirations, home is a projection of personal life. Aalto's houses, on the other hand, contain a benevolent margin for unconstrained and liberated life. Even the detailing and furnishing, light fittings, and everyday objects he designed project this relaxed and unrestrained ambience, and Aalto's designs belong to the few popularly accepted pieces of uncompromisingly modern design after the decades of Michael Thonet's popular chairs, more than a century earlier.

Toward the end of the 1920s, Aalto turned enthusiastically and abruptly to continental functionalism, the modern style that had entered the Nordic countries primarily through the Stockholm Exhibition of 1930. He turned into an

Aalto, furniture designs for Artek, 1930–1950s. Aalto's designs for furniture, light fittings, and glassware exude a relaxed, intimate, and tactile ambience regardless of their uncompromised aesthetics.

ardent spokesman for the modern lifestyle and rationalized and aesthetically restrained architecture. One of the ideals of early modernism was the concept of the minimum dwelling. For a while Aalto preached the idea of the perfectly rationalized dwelling, emphasizing that the minimum apartment must be part of a larger collective of architecture.[12] In 1930 he designed and helped to organize the Minimum Apartment exhibition in Helsinki, largely in collaboration with his talented architect wife Aino. In an essay published in conjunction with the exhibition, Aalto explains his novel ideas:

> No family can live in one room, and not even two if it has children. But any family can live quite well in an area of the same size if that area is divided with a view to the life of the family and the activities of its members. A home is an area that forms a sheltered space for eating, sleeping, working, and playing. These biodynamic forms must serve as the basis for internal divisions of a home, not obsolete symmetrical axes and standard rooms dictated by facade architecture.... Movable, versatile furniture makes a small apartment larger: The gist of the method discussed here therefore essentially consists of making the apartment larger and increasing its potential.[13]

The architect called for a scientific attitude to design, looking to science to define the requirements and standards of the home.[14] Aalto's enthusiasm in the rationalist approach, which he also called "new realism" and "non-synthetic architecture," was, however, short-lived. Already five years later he sought to redefine the concept of rationalism to allow for a more humane design. In a lecture titled "Rationalism and Man" (1935) he stated:

> We have admitted...that objects that can rightly be called rational often suffer from flagrant inhumanity.... Thus we might say that one way to produce a more humane built environment is to extend our definition of rationalism.[15]

Around the time he gave this lecture, Aalto set out to do exactly what he deliberated on: to extend the idea of rationalism into a psychological, physiological, and organic direction. His purely rationalist and emotionally cool projects for dwellings and houses, such as the Standard Apartment Building in Turku (1927), are followed by projects of warm domesticity, comfort, and mental rootedness. A sense of soft romanticism replaces rationalist reduction and purity. The strict modernist geometry and white surfaces turn into a complex interplay of spaces, forms, materials, and textures. The house as a techno-rational artifact is replaced by multi-thematic and emotive settings that are a blend of modernity and a sense of historical rootedness and tradition. The earlier visual emphasis is replaced by a tactile intimacy, universality by regional features, consistency by improvisation, logic by play, and clarity by a sense of mystery. Even his standardized products were based on a need for variation, as "formalism is inhuman to the highest degree."[16]

These new characteristics first emerge in the Aalto House in Helsinki (1935–36), the architects' combined residence and studio. Keeping in mind that this is the house of an architect of thirty-seven years of age, known for his radicalism and desire to shock the bourgeoisie, the domestic warmth and traditionalism, combined with relaxed and unpretentious modern features, is most unexpected. The house speaks convincingly of the architect's maturity.

The undisputed masterpiece among Aalto's house designs is the Villa Mairea in Noormarkku, Finland, designed as an *opus con amore* for Harry and Maire Gullichsen, the architects' intimate friends, patrons, and collaborators. The project marks Aalto's final separation from the strict aesthetic ideals of functionalism. The house combines images of continental modernism, traditional Finnish farm vernacular, and Japanese aesthetic culture in a collage manner into a uniquely rich and symphonic piece of residential architecture. "The goal was to avoid artificial architectural rhythm in the building without giving up pure form as long as it could be obtained in harmony with the structure or with an increased use of materials and surface treatments that are inherently pleasing to the senses," Aalto explained.[17]

The Villa Mairea is also a rare synthesis of architecture and art. In addition to housing the clients' fine collection of mostly modern continental artworks, modern art at large was a source of inspiration for the architect, as he revealed in a project description for a Finnish magazine:

> In this building the designer sought to apply a special concept of form connected to modern painting. He believes that modern painting gives a building and a home a deeper and ultimately more human material and formal accent than an ornament designed as an architectural appendage can.[18]

Aalto himself practiced painting and made sculptural objects ever since his youth, and several great painters, such as Georges Braque, Fernand Léger, and Max Ernst, were among his personal friends. His affinity with painting helps to understand the new logic of his painterly architecture, which creates a sequence of ambiences and moods rather than articulations of spatial geometry.

Although the house is a uniquely crafted setting for a wealthy industrialist couple, Aalto himself presented it, rather surprisingly, as an experiment of wider social value:

> An architectural assignment based on an individual lifestyle, instinct and conception of culture can have far-reaching social significance in the

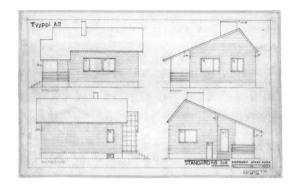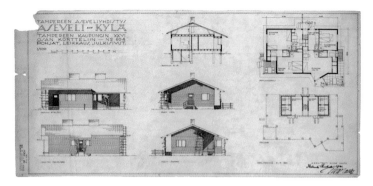

Aalto, wooden standard housing, Varkaus, Savonmäki District, Finland, 1937. The house types have a traditional appearance although Aalto designed purely modernist dwellings at the time, such as the Kauttua Terrace House (Kauttua, 1937–38).

Aalto, type house for the Asevelikylä village of ex-service men, Tampere, Finland, 1943

long run.... The individual architectural assignment can be treated as a laboratory experiment of sorts, in which things can be done that would be impossible with present-day mass production, and those experiments can spread further and eventually become available to one and all as production methods advance.[19]

At the time that the Villa Mairea was being furnished, at the end of 1939, the Winter War between Finland and the Soviet Union broke out. The war threw Aalto and other architects from their modern utopian aspirations back to basic issues of survival and dwelling, and the need to develop efficient, variable, and cheap housing systems to settle the numerous families who had lost their homes during the devastating war.

Aalto had designed housing areas for Finnish industries as early as the 1930s. In addition to modernist housing types at the Sunila Pulp Mill (1936–38) and the Standard Terrace House at Kauttua (1937–38), he also developed several types of wooden worker's houses. The modernist Sunila housing area includes a cluster of hip-roofed standardized wood houses of the same type as those tested earlier by the A. Ahlström Company in Varkaus. These so-called A-System houses were designed with the intention that the company would supply the wood material required to execute the standard drawings for self-build houses.

During his research professorship at the Massachusetts Institute of Technology immediately after the Winter War in 1940, Aalto and his students continued to work on the complex aspects of system housing. His vision was to make Finland a laboratory of modern housing, and he sought to raise American funds for this enterprise to design and build "An American Town in Finland," a model town using advanced industrial methods. Due to the Continuation War of 1941–45, Aalto was, however, obliged to return abruptly to Finland, where he was put in charge of the Office for Reconstruction, an institution set up by the Finnish Association of Architects for the research and design of simple, efficient, and economic self-build housing. He was also responsible for directing the housing operation of the A. Ahlström Company. The resulting industrialized system was called the AA-System House and utilized the newly available insulation technology of the 1930s, to create a wood-frame structure that was thermally suited to the severe Finnish climate. It represented a significant shift from the traditional Finnish housing construction of horizontally laid logs covered by wooden boards.

After the early 1950s, Aalto became engaged in an ever increasing number of public commissions in his own country and abroad. As a consequence he had less time to design houses, and the world-famous architect and academician was probably also considered too authoritarian and expensive by individual

An unexecuted project for artist/
designer Roberto Sambonet (1955)
with a Mediterranean ambience

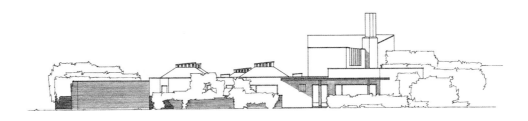

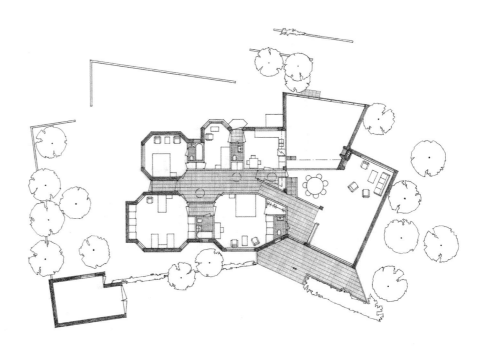

Villa Erica (1970), an unexecuted
house project that would have
been Aalto's most complex and
luxurious private house

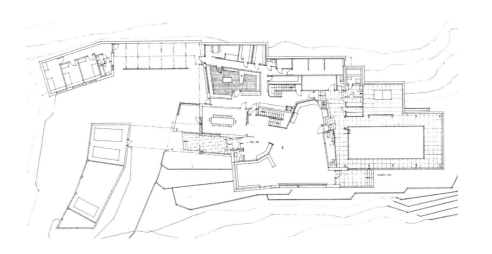

clients. Aalto did, however, continue to execute houses even during his two last decades, such as the houses for Joonas Kokkonen, the composer, in Järvenpää (1967–69), and for Göran Schildt, his biographer, in Tammisaari (Villa Skeppet, 1969–70). He also designed interesting unexecuted projects, such as a house for his Italian designer friend Roberto Sambonet (1955) near Milan, and the Villa Erica (1970) designed for the industrialist Adriano Olivetti's niece Erica and her husband Marino Bin in Monsalieri near Turin in Italy.

By far the most ambitious of Aalto's executed postwar houses is the Maison Carré (1956–59), the residence of the famous and wealthy French art collector and dealer Louis Carré in Bazoches-sur-Guyonne outside Paris. This house returns to many of the themes that Aalto had developed in the Villa Mairea twenty years earlier as well as in his numerous public buildings, such as the contemporaneous Church of the Three Crosses in Vuoksenniska (1955–58), which is reflected in the section and light fittings of the Maison Carré's entrance hall. Aalto and his second wife Elissa designed the house down to the smallest detail, including a number of custom-made furniture pieces and light fittings. Like the Villa Mairea, the Maison Carré is subtly tailored to the requests and desires of the client. While it is unmistakably of Aalto's hand and projects an ambience of the architect's Finnish modernity, it also echoes characteristics of French culture.

One of Aalto's special talents as a designer was indeed his exceptional sense of empathy that enabled him to design a luxurious home for a world-famous art dealer, or a modest house for his taxi driver. He could also shift his design style from an urban and refined character to a rustic and vernacular ambience when building outside of city centers. Sigfried Giedion described Aalto's empathetic character admiringly:

> One cannot speak about Aalto the architect without speaking about Aalto the man. People are at least as important to him as architecture. Aalto is interested in every human being, in each of their particular desires and experiences, no matter where they come from or to what social class they belong. He draws incentive and stimulation from contacts with men of varied callings, much as James Joyce did. Indeed, Aalto cannot set foot outside his door without becoming involved in some human episode. He approaches people directly and without inhibitions.[20]

Regardless of his numerous friends and clients in the highest circles of society, both in his own country and abroad, Aalto repeatedly spoke of "the little man," or the "man at his weakest," an individual without wealth and power, as the architect's ultimate client.[21] His empathetic skills were combined with a sense of realism. He once claimed: "Realism usually provides the strongest stimulus to my imagination."[22] It was Alvar Aalto's unique capacity to combine rational judgment with intuition, realism with idealization, and persuasion with compassion that made him one of the most important architects of residential designs in the twentieth century.

Map of Sites

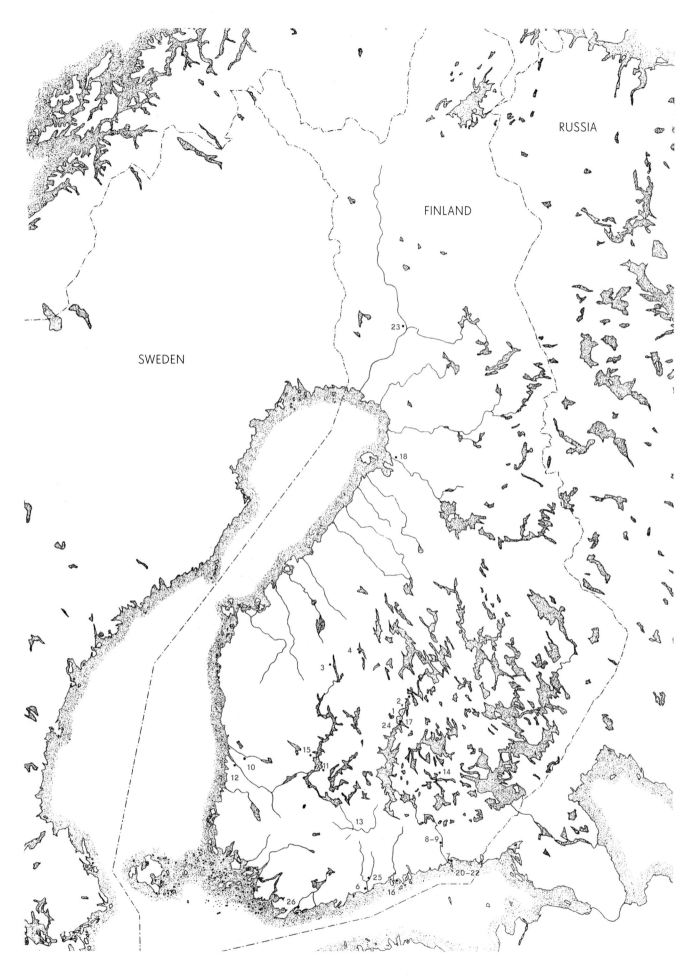

RUSSIA

FINLAND

SWEDEN

The 1920s: Classicism and Vernacular

In the 1920s Finland was a young nation struggling with many societal and economical challenges. Having gained its independence from the Russian Empire in 1917, it went through a civil war the following year. Nonetheless, the country recovered rapidly, and the latter half of the decade introduced modernity into Finnish culture, especially in the cities, while in rural areas daily life still remained largely unchanged. In general, the era was characterized by dynamic renewal and political tensions.

Alvar Aalto graduated as an architect from the University of Technology in Helsinki in 1921 and moved back to his hometown, Jyväskylä, in central Finland to start his first office there. The 1920s marked significant phases in his life: in addition to starting a career, he married architect Aino Marsio (1894–1949) in 1924 and moved to Turku in south-west Finland in 1927, where he designed his first seminal competition proposals.

The four houses by Aalto discussed in this chapter all share elements of Nordic classicism in their architectural expression and are characterized by their solid volumes and typical neoclassical details, such as columns and garlands. It was only in the late 1920s that the architect moved toward modernism, most notably with the Turun Sanomat Building (Turku, 1929–30) and the Paimio Tuberculosis Sanatorium (Paimio, 1929–33).

opposite
**Terho Manner
House, entrance
hall staircase**

Nuora House

Jyväskylä, Finland
1922

The alteration of the Nuora House dates from the early years of Aalto's practice in Jyväskylä. Typical for the architect's first commissions, it was a renovation, which consisted of adding one floor to an existing building. The house had a small bakery and cafe on the ground floor, to which Aalto added three small studio apartments on the second floor.[1] This combination of functions resulted in four entrances on three sides of the house: three leading to the cafe and bakery and one upstairs. The predominant element of the main facade is a large balcony with an arcade motif, which can be seen as one version of the loggia theme of the Italian Renaissance, an important inspiration for Aalto in the 1920s. This theme of an intermediate space between inside and out would evolve in later projects to more complex combinations of spatial sequences. One modification, for example, lies in the essential role the main staircase plays in several Aalto houses.

The exterior of the Nuora House is characteristic for classicist Finnish architecture of the 1920s. The wooden vertical cladding links it to vernacular buildings, while some of its neo-classical decorative motifs, such as the stylized wooden columns, appear somewhat exaggerated. The capitals are especially oversized compared to the otherwise modest look of the house. The interior spaces are conventional with separate small rooms.

In the Ostrobothnian region of Finland, where Aalto was born and spent his early childhood, two-story wooden houses were a common residential building type, especially during the late nineteenth century. The size of the houses expressed the wealth of a family and household and they often had classicist details. In the larger projects of the Alatalo Manor (1923–24) and the Terho Manner House (1923–26), Aalto continued to combine traditional vernacular Finnish farmhouse forms and motifs with elegant 1920s classicist details.

opposite
**The Nuora House from the west.
The tower of the 1920s Taulumäki
church by architect Elsi Borg is
visible on the right.**

below
**Facade drawings
and plans**

opposite top
Main entrance

opposite bottom
South entrance

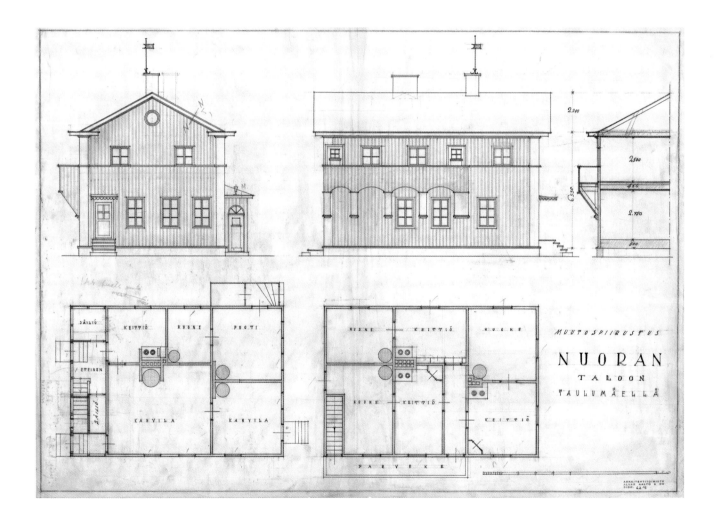

top
Master bedroom

bottom
Living room

opposite
**View of the original stove
in the living room**

Alatalo Manor

Tarvaala, Laukaa, Finland
1923–24

In the design of the Alatalo Manor Aalto's Ostrobothnian roots are clearly noticeable, although one should bear in mind that classical features were admired and cultivated among other Finnish architects during the 1920s as well. The Alatalo farm was a wealthy estate in central Finland, located some twenty miles north of Jyväskylä. Its owner, Otto Ollikainen, financially supported by his father-in-law, commissioned Aalto to design a main building for the farm in 1923, but, experiencing personal troubles, he developed a drinking problem and eventually lost most of his property. The house was therefore never completely finished, but for many years was owned by a local parish and rented out to tenants who caused damage. The present owners renovated the house in the early 1980s according to the original drawings.[2]

The Alatalo Manor and its more recent outbuildings are surrounded by an open landscape of fields. In the house, different styles meet: its compact symmetrical two-story volume has roots in neo-classical architecture and Finnish farmhouses, while its low, hipped roof is reminiscent of nineteenth-century wooden townhouses. The stucco facades of the main entrance vestibule and the garden veranda contrast with the vertical wooden cladding of the main volume. The unusual combination of wooden and stucco facade elements was favored in 1920s classicist architecture for its surprising and articulating effect. Aalto would use similar combinations in many of his later houses, including his own home in Helsinki (1936) and the Villa Mairea (1937–39) in Noormarkku. Most of the house's few architectural accents, such as the circular windows and articulated trim around the six-pane windows, are concentrated on the garden facade, where the veranda, with its large windows, gives the house a more open character.

In plan a longitudinal hall divides the interior into two separate groups: on the left, when entering the house, are the everyday functional spaces, such as a kitchen and bathroom. Adjacent to the kitchen is a version of the traditional Finnish tupa, a large dining-living room that could be used for several purposes. The other side of the house consists of the large spaces of the formal dining room and the owner's room, as well as the somewhat smaller master bedroom and children's room.

The hall is unusually long, extending all the way from the front entrance to the garden veranda, linking the two ends of the house. Aalto seemed to refer to this hall when he wrote in his seminal essay "From Doorstep to Living Room" in 1926:

> One of the possible forms I should like to indicate is the long-despised corridor. As a part of the entrance to a house, it offers undreamed-of aesthetic potential, as it is a

natural coordinator of the inner rooms, and permits the use of a bold, monumental linear scale, even in small buildings.[3]

The almost public character of the hall was emphasized in the original drawings with the use of a coffered ceiling and a solemn composition of rifles and moose horns on the wall. It is not known whether Aalto intended the present bare log walls to be exposed. The otherwise refined articulation and detailing in the drawings indicate that the walls might have been meant to be clad with horizontal boards.

top
**Detailed sections
of the hall**

bottom
First-floor plan

opposite top left
**The symmetrical volume
of the Alatalo Manor in
the rural landscape**

opposite top right
Garden facade

opposite bottom
Main entrance facade

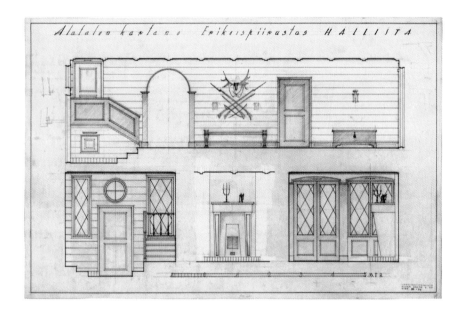

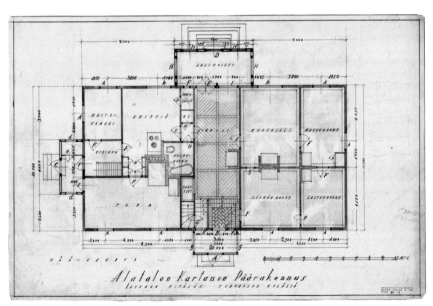

below
View from the hall

opposite
The sunny garden veranda features window frames typical for Aalto's 1920s buildings.

Terho Manner House

Töysä, Finland
1923–26

The monumental character of the Terho Manner House is reminiscent of nineteenth-century Finnish manor houses, characterized by their symmetrical compositions and outbuildings flanking the courtyards. Engineer Terho Manner was a cousin of Aalto's mother, who, like Aalto's father, worked as a surveyor. He was also the leader of the local defense corps and thus had a link with the land-owning class that had recently won the civil war.[4] The project for Manner and his family preceded Aalto's later house commissions in several ways: Aalto would design the majority of his private houses for relatives or friends, although he sometimes knew his clients from other projects, typically industrial commissions. And just as the Manner House included offices for the engineer's work as a surveyor, the combination of dwelling and work continued to be a motif in later Aalto houses.

Located in a lake landscape in central Finland, the Manner House has a dominant position on a sloping hillside with a terraced stairway descending down to the shore. At the same time the group of buildings—the house and the two large wings flanking it—communicates with the surroundings. The lower symmetrical wings repeat the form of the main house, all three facing the lake with neo-classical pediments, and the courtyard opens to the lake in a gesture of welcome. Originally, there was also a sauna building and a swimming pavilion

on the tip of a long wooden jetty, but both were demolished in the 1950s.

Despite the importance of the lake facade visitors arrive at the house from a different angle. The driveway passes a small garden pavilion, reminiscent of a classical temple, and approaches the main entrance and its imposing Empire colonnade from the side. Turns and shifts interested Aalto from the start of his career, and many of his later houses would repeat this theme. They are a part of the ritual of arriving, moving through and experiencing a sequence of spaces.

The storage wings play an important role in defining the front courtyard, which is further demarcated by the natural topography of the site and a hedge planted where the land slopes toward the lake. The hierarchy of the buildings is emphasized with variations of colonnades, from the monumental porch of the main building—which appears some-what exaggerated in comparison with the rest of the house—to the elegant garden pavilion, to the almost humorous colonnade elements on the storage doors.

Just as in the Alatalo Manor, the hall is the focal point of the Terho Manner House. It serves the practical needs of circulation but also visually and spatially connects the surrounding rooms with each other and with a view to the lake. The octagonal space opens in four directions, leading to the most

opposite
**Stone steps lead up from the lakeside
garden to the main entrance.**

important rooms, including the dining hall, combined salon and library, and master bedroom, as well as out to the porch and lake. Articulated with slender columns and arches, the hall has a double-layered character: behind the arcaded loggia, shallow recesses alternate with deeper openings, transforming it into a symbolic open-air space underneath the roof of the home.[5] Aalto would play with the concept of such outdoor-indoor spaces throughout his career.

Another favorite theme of the architect's was the main staircase as both a functional and transitional element that is of great importance to the spatial experience. In the Terho Manner House a meandering staircase leads from the hall to the second floor. Its arched opening and balustrade railings belong to the vocabulary of classicism, while its winding spaces invite visitors to step further: the staircase is at the same time visible and hidden. The kitchen wing can be accessed both from the hall and through one of the house's two side entrances; the other one leads to Manner's office, which was, like the parlor (the present living room) semi-public. The combination of work and home also included rooms for some of Manner's employees on the second floor.[6]

In spite of the building's strict external symmetry, room sizes vary according to their function and significance. The elegant dining hall, with its exposed ceiling beams and double doorways painted with an arch motif, is the largest space. Here and in the other rooms of the house, colors play a seminal role in the interior design, creating a different character for each space, with hues of green, blue,

ochre, and Pompeian red. Special treatment was given to a guest room on the second floor, whose log walls were left exposed in the manner of an Ostrobothnian-style farmhouse room, also including a traditional open fireplace in the corner, pointing to the family's regional roots. It can serve as an example of how Aalto combined vernacular and high culture in many of his houses.[7] The architect had originally designed custom fireplaces for most of the rooms but in the end standard tiled stoves were used.[8]

In his seminal essay "From Doorstep to Living Room," written at the time the Alatalo Manor was completed, Aalto stated the importance of gardens in residential architecture:

> The garden (or courtyard) belongs to our home just as much as any of the rooms. Let the step from the kitchen garden to the rooms provide a much smaller contrast than the one from the road or street to the garden.[9]

In the Terho Manner House, this connection between the interior and exterior spaces is expressed through hedges and flowerbeds that line the stone steps and the straight pathway leading down from the veranda to the lakeshore. Designed by Paul Olsson (1890–1973), a notable Finnish landscape architect, who was involved in several other Aalto houses, in collaboration with the architect, the garden combines cultural, man-made landscape with natural forests and fields around it, a feature that would also be an important element in the Villa Mairea.[10]

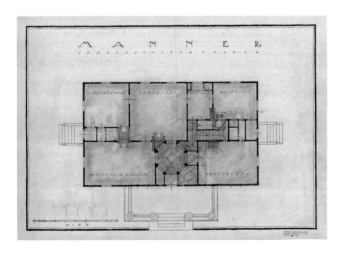

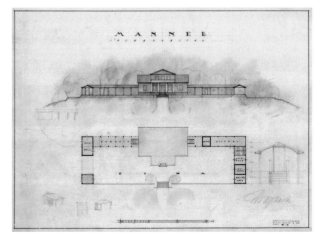

below
**Living room with Pompeian
red walls and a white
glazed tile stove**

left
Exposed log walls and an
open fireplace define
the Ostrobothnian room
on the second floor.

right
The octagonal hall with
a round glazed tile stove
in the corner is the heart of
the house. Slender columns
with arches define the
space. Through the center
arch a view opens to the
dining room.

right
**The arch motif of the
hall continues in the
dining room.**

Villa Vekara

Karstula, Finland
1924–25

Villa Vekara, commissioned by agronomist Emil Vekara, who in the 1920s lived in the house adjacent to Aalto's architectural office in Jyväskylä, was the first summer house Aalto designed.[11] The building is small, with a living room and a kitchen on the ground floor and two small bedrooms upstairs. Located near a lake on rocky terrain in central Finland, the site's topographical conditions were challenging because of a steep slope, and the original plan was mirrored to fit the terrain better.[12] Aalto added variation and asymmetry to the simple saddleback-roofed volume by using a different roof angle on the lakeside porch. A loggia motif with a low barrel-vaulted ceiling articulates both the entrance porch and the larger lakeside veranda. Other elegant accents include luscious balustrades in the spirit of the Italian Renaissance, while the use of red ochre paint and exposed log walls is reminiscent of Finnish vernacular traditions. Both in the Nuora House and in the Villa Vekara, Aalto reveals a kind of playfulness by adding fancy high-culture elements to a traditional frame. Villa Vekara's interior with its hewn log walls and exposed beam structures has a traditional atmosphere with intricate woodwork, seen especially in the staircase detailing with its cut baluster forms and cofferings. This kind of attention to details is later evident even in Aalto's most modest standard houses.

opposite
View of the house from the lakeside

top
**Plans, facade, and
section**

bottom
**Detailed drawings of the
doors and windows**

opposite top
**The loggia-like lakeside
veranda features a low
barrel vault and balusters.**

opposite bottom
**Entrance porch with
balusters**

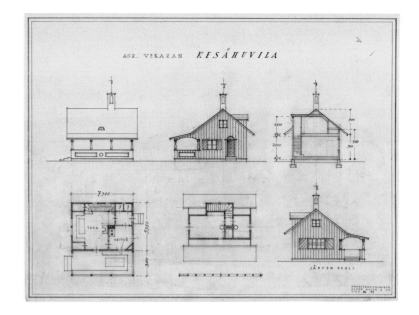

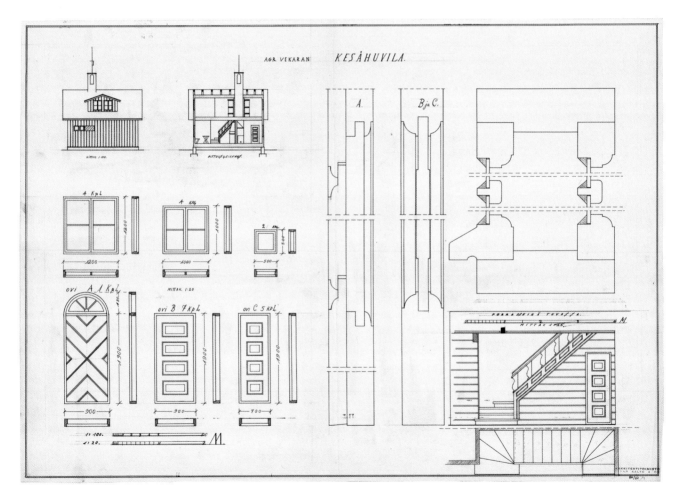

below
Detail of the staircase

opposite
The *tupa* room with its log walls and exposed wooden structure

The 1930s: Private Villas and Company Housing

In the early 1930s Finland was overshadowed by the Great Depression. By the mid-1930s, though, the economy began to improve, and despite extreme political tensions in Europe the country was looking toward a brighter future. The paper industry was flourishing, and its role in Finland's economic growth became essential.

For Aalto's career the 1930s meant a breakthrough in many ways. He gained international reputation with his wooden furniture as well as with his first modern buildings, the Turun Sanomat Building and the Paimio Tuberculosis Sanatorium. Aalto also helped convey the image of Finland to the international scene with his exhibition pavilions for the Paris International Exhibition of 1936–37 and for the New York World Fair of 1939.

Decisive commissions for the Aalto office in the 1930s came from the industrial sector. The growth of wood industry companies in the 1930s resulted in a need for new plants and residential communities, and it was during this time that Aalto established firm connections with several companies that would provide work for his office during the next two decades. The most important tie Alvar and Aino Aalto established was that to the A. Ahlström company and its general director Harry Gullichsen and his wife Maire Gullichsen (neé Ahlström). The Gullichsens became the Aaltos' close friends in the mid-1930s, and while the professional relationship resulted in numerous commissions for industrial buildings and communities, the personal friendship led to the design of the Villa Mairea. An important collaborative effort of the Aaltos and the Gullichsens was the establishment of the furniture company Artek in 1935.[1]

While Aalto's 1920s houses were representative of Nordic classicism, the architect became an enthusiastic exponent of functionalism in the later years of the decade. In the early 1930s Aalto still favored standardization in design, but he soon began to strive for a more humane approach, and nature and its biological standardization became the main model for his architecture. From the mid-1930s onwards he brought wood into the material palette of his buildings, softening and enriching the stark white volumes. He also started to use free, undulating, or amoeboid forms in canopies, interior surfaces, and in his designs for glass vases and furniture.

opposite
Villa Mairea,
main entrance

Villa Tammekann

Tartu, Estonia
1932–33

Villa Tammekann, located in the old university town of Tartu in Estonia, was the first project Aalto realized outside of Finland. August Tammekann, a professor of geography, had met Aalto in Turku in the early 1930s. At that time the effects of the Depression were still felt in Finland, and in his conversations with the professor, Aalto had mentioned the lack of commissions since the completion of the Paimio Sanatorium.[2] When Tammekann decided to build a home for his family in March 1932, he wrote Aalto, asking for a proposal for a modern villa in a verdant single-family home area, where many members of Tartu's intelligentsia lived.[3] During the next few months, the two exchanged many letters to discuss and refine the design. The Tammekanns had very specific wishes for the arrangement of rooms and clearly stated the needs of the family, discussing everything from the height of the first floor to the sizes of windows.[4] Among other things, August Tammekann's wife, Irene Tammekann, insisted on a room of her own that provided evening sunlight and a window facing west: "I am forced to inform you that if I do not get my own room and the kind of room that I myself want, then the house will not be built."[5]

The project proceeded quickly, and after the building permit was issued in mid-July, construction began immediately.[6] Although the main idea of the building and many details were realized according to Aalto's plans, some essential changes happened along the way. The most serious was the thickness of the walls, which had to be increased from 18 inches to massive brick walls of 25.5 inches, due to technical problems and the unavailability of some materials in Estonia in the early 1930s. Thus the proportions and dimensions of the spaces were altered, and room sizes dramatically reduced. When Aalto learned of the decision, he, quite cordially, wrote to complain that he was not informed of this problem, explaining that he would have revised the plan if he had known.[7] Technical problems continued with the flat roof, which leaked from the beginning.[8]

The family moved into the half-finished house in the spring of 1933, and even in early 1935, many parts of the house were still incomplete, including the balconies and the facade finishes as well as parts of the interior.[9] Financial problems in Estonia and restrictions for payments abroad also caused delays in the payment of the architect's salary.

Villa Tammekann's functionalistic appearance incorporates typical features of early international modernism: with its flat roof, simple cubic volume, white stucco walls, horizontal windows, terraces, and balconies, it is reminiscent of Aalto's design for the chief physician's house at the Paimio Sanatorium. Despite the problems during construction the room arrangement basically followed the architect's original design. A spacious living room with large

opposite
View of the house from the garden

windows opening onto the garden was at the center of the house. A fireplace underneath the strip windows was to be the central element of the room, so that people sitting around it could see both the fire and the trees in the garden at the same time, strengthening the unity of the interior and exterior spaces. However, the fireplace remained unbuiltuntil the present owner renovated the building inthe 1990s.

The living room and its adjacent spaces— a study-library and a dining room—form an interconnected group running the length of the house. Like many other Aalto houses, the villa has a separate office for Professor Tammekann with an adjacent small storage room for maps. The house's modern interior elements include a kitchen designed according to the Frankfurt kitchen principles, intended to improve efficiency for the housewife. This part of the house experienced the most changes due to the thickening of the walls. On the second floor were the bedrooms and children's room.

The story of the Villa Tammekann took a dramatic turn with the beginning of World War Two, which led to the occupation of Estonia, among other Baltic States, by the Soviet Union. The Tammekann family fled to Finland in the summer of 1940 and would never return to live in Tartu. During the Soviet era the house was divided into several apartments, and in the 1950s, the flat roof was replaced by a hipped roof. These changes, together with bad maintenance over several decades, brought the house into critical condition by the late 1990s. The Turku University Foundation bought the building in 1998 and carried out a thorough renovation and restoration project during the next two years, which included the construction of features that were part of Aalto's original design but had never been realized for financial reasons: a terrace with a pergola, a garage, and the living room fireplace beneath the strip windows.[10] Since 2000 the building has housed the Granö Centre of the universities of Turku and Tartu.

villa tammekann

opposite left
**Aino Aalto at Villa Tammekann
with the Aaltos' 1929 Buick**

opposite right
**Perspective of the living room.
The fireplace underneath the
strip window was the main
element of the room.**

top
First-floor plan

bottom
**The south-facing terrace
with pergola**

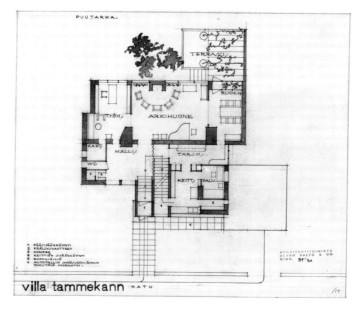

top
Second-floor hall. The small table and stackable stool were designed for the Paimio Sanatorium in 1932. In the 1920s and early 1930s Aalto used lamps by Danish designer Poul Henningsen (1894–1967) in his houses, such as the wall lamps from the 1930s shown here.

bottom
Entrance hall. The PH 5 lamp model by Henningsen is from 1958. The coat rack was designed by Anna Maija Jaatinen for Artek in 1964.

below
The kitchen was designed according to the Frankfurt kitchen principles.

right
Living room. The tea trolley and armchairs were designed by Aalto in 1936 and exhibited at the Milan Triennial. The floor lamps were custom-made for Aalto's National Pensions Institute in the late 1950s.

The Aalto House

Helsinki, Finland
1935–36

In 1933, in the middle of the Depression years, Aino and Alvar Aalto and their two children moved to Helsinki. For the architects the capital offered more work opportunities than the smaller town of Turku. During the first years, the Aaltos lived in two different apartments in Helsinki before buying a plot on Riihitie in the municipality of Munkkiniemi from the M. G. Stenius company, the principal landowner of the area.[11] At that time Munkkiniemi was just outside of Helsinki and sparsely inhabited. In this almost rural landscape Aino and Alvar Aalto designed and built their modern home and office. The plans for the house were finished in July 1935. Construction progressed swiftly, and the Aalto family moved into their new home in August 1936.[12]

The Aalto House incorporates many aspects of the architects' ideals for home design and central concepts of dwelling. The first encounter with the house shows an almost entirely enclosed street facade, with only one window (that of the office reception) overlooking the street. The enclosure is further emphasized with a high brick wall, which surrounds the kitchen entrance area. The main entrance is tucked into a corner of the wall. The composition of the lime-washed, lightly rendered brick walls and dark-stained vertical wood boarding dominates the view.

Whereas the Villa Tammekann still followed the straightforward aesthetic ideals of late-1920s and early-1930s international modernism, the Aalto House has a more sensitive and intimate approach. Though it has often been compared with Walter Gropius's Masters' Houses at the Bauhaus (Dessau, 1925–26)—both in its plan and its external appearance—the harmonious relation it forms with the surroundings and its atmosphere of domesticity give it a warmer and more humane character.

The house includes a two-story office wing, which on the exterior is articulated with white-rendered brickwork and white-painted wood boarding. The office or studio is spacious, with a narrow interior balcony that was used as an extra work space, for example for scale model building. A large atelier window facing northwest gives light to the space, and a corner window opens a pleasant view into the garden. The busiest years for Aalto were from the late 1930s until the early 1950s, when several large projects, including various industrial areas and buildings, the pavilions for the international exhibitions, and the Villa Mairea, were on the architect's drawing tables. After a separate studio was built in 1955, the office wing served as a private studio for Aalto and his second wife, Elissa.

The residential part of the house was divided into the semi-public spaces of the living and dining rooms with utilities on the first floor and the private rooms—the bedrooms and a guestroom—on the second floor. This division for different levels of

opposite

**View of the house from
the south**

privacy is accentuated on the exterior, where the most private spaces have a dark-colored wooden envelope, while the living and dining rooms at the heart of the house open generously onto the garden with large windows. These rooms also served as intermediate spaces between the office and family life. The almost non-existing border is a wooden sliding door in the living room: if it is open, there is a direct visual connection to the office; if it is closed, you can still hear the voices behind it. This triad of dining-living-working spaces can be found in almost all Aalto houses. The individual rooms can be treated as separate units in some cases but most often the architect united them into a continuous sequence of spaces.

The second floor exhibits another of Aalto's favorite themes—the central hall, which in this case was also used as a family breakfast room. A fireplace gives it a cozy atmosphere. The hall leads to the roof terrace, which can also be accessed from the office wing. It was a symbol of a modern, healthy life, and was used for recreation and gymnastic exercises, while the garden was especially important to Aino Aalto, who specified a list of plants on the earliest garden plans. Cherry, apple, and rowan trees were planted next to the existing pine trees, and the slope was terraced with stone retaining walls. A stone-paved yard with an adjacent small pool provided spaces for relaxation and contemplation.

Numerous details in the Aalto House illustrate how important a good everyday environment was for the architects. Wall coverings, such as the bast textile in the studio and the moleskin fabric in the dining hall, serve both an acoustic purpose and are aesthetically pleasing. All main rooms in the house had fireplaces—a trace from the past, reminiscent of people sitting together around the fire, and also a necessity in the winter time as the only isolation of the wooden walls was a combination of Insulite boards and air. The built-in furnishings were designed especially for the house, but key pieces,

still existing, were bought already for previous homes, including Aino's grand piano and Alvar's favorite armchair.

The structure of the building consisted mostly of steel columns and reinforced concrete components, but also of traditional brick walls.[13] Both the interior and exterior treatments show sensuous variety. The brick structure is visible underneath the lime layer and the wooden panels on the facade are painted either dark brown or white, marking the difference between the office and residential part. This emphasis on the surface structure and natural materials became an important element of Aalto's buildings in the 1930s, resulting in a richer palette.

Although the Aalto House has many features typical for the time, such as a flat roof, cubic volumes, and a roof terrace, it is also strongly rooted in the best of Finnish traditions. Art historian and architect Gustaf Strengell (1878–1937), who wrote with great enthusiasm about Aalto's first functionalist buildings and was a significant supporter of Aalto, visited the house on a summer afternoon in 1937. According to Göran Schildt, he delivered the finest criticism Aalto ever received of his home when he said: "I just visited the Seurasaari museum to see the Niemelä farm. Now I should like to see the modern Niemelä farm once more."[14] By this, Strengell wanted to express that he understood the Aalto House to be a part of a longer continuum and that the best of a tradition or roots can be articulated in modern architecture.

Family life in the Aalto House went on in tranquility until the late 1940s, when Aino Aalto became seriously ill and died in 1949. A second phase for Aalto started in 1952 when he and Elsa Mäkiniemi (1922–1994), later Elissa Aalto, were married. They both lived in the house until their deaths, in 1976 (Alvar Aalto) and in 1994 (Elissa Aalto), respectively. Today the Aalto House is owned by the Alvar Aalto Foundation, which maintains it as a museum.

top
Aino and Alvar Aalto in the studio, 1941

middle left
Sketch of the south facade

middle right
Aalto in the living room, 1941. On the table is the first edition of Ernest Hemingway's *For Whom the Bell Tolls*, 1940.

bottom left
First-floor plan

bottom right
Second-floor plan

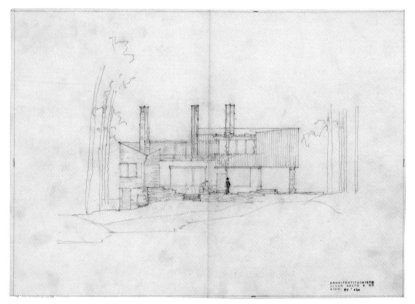

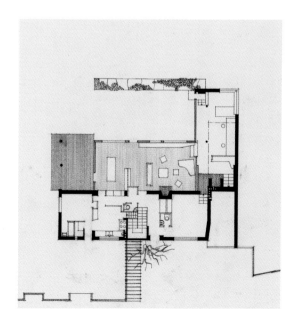

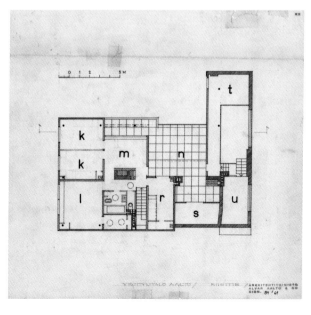

below
**View of the studio
from the garden**

opposite
Studio

left

The second-floor hall was used as a family and breakfast room. Maire Gullichsen designed the table lamp, while the pendant lamp, PH 3, is by Poul Henningsen. The floor lamp, Angel's Wing, was designed for the National Pensions Institute in the 1950s. The carpet is a prototype for the Maison Carré and was designed by Elissa Aalto in 1957.

right

The Aaltos' daughter's bedroom

opposite

Dining room with Italian revival–style chairs bought by the Aaltos during their honeymoon in Italy in 1924. The pendant lamp, type number A203 fom 1953, was designed for the Säynätsalo Town Hall. The chairs at either end of the table are by Aino Aalto (1940s).

right
The living room with Alvar's
favorite armchair and Aino's
grand piano (covered by the
fabric Siena, designed by
Alvar in 1954) also features a
low tobacco table (a prototype
from 1929–30) and a floor
lamp designed for the Maison
Carré in 1959.

Kantola, Manager's Residence

Sunila Company
Kotka, Finland
1936–37

Southeastern Finland has been the country's dominating timber industry region since the late nineteenth century. First sawmills and later cellulose, paper, and board mills were located along the area's lakes and rivers. Kymijoki, the region's largest river, served as a source of clean water needed in the industrial processes and as a vital transportation route.

The Sunila pulp mill was founded in 1936 by five forestry companies in order to produce pulp for paper mills, and Aalto was commissioned to design both the industrial complex and the surrounding residential area. His master plan placed the production facilities on a small island in the sea, at the southernmost point of the Kymijoki waterway, while the housing area is on the mainland nearby on a somewhat hilly terrain grown with pine trees. Apartment buildings and row houses were distributed freely in the landscape, bearing in mind the optimal orientation to the sunlight and the topography, with dwellings for the upper management sited close to the mill and seashore. Staff hierarchy is visible in the different types of residential buildings: a single-family house for the manager, two types of terraced houses for the engineers and foremen, and apartment blocks for the workers. Nevertheless, the functionalist character of the houses unites them architecturally, and there is no clear division between the different social strata.

Named after Lauri Kanto, who was the general manager of the Sunila mill and in charge of the construction of the factory in the 1930s, Kantola, the manager's residence, is sited somewhat separate from the other dwellings in the area. The approach to the house passes the foremen's and engineers' row houses and leads diagonally to the building, where a stonewall marks the yard area in the otherwise continuous forest landscape. The house is oriented toward the garden and the sea and has typical features of the 1930s, such as a flat roof and clear compact volume. The facade's light plaster surface leaves the texture of the bricks visible underneath. Their off-white color contrasts with the use of yellow brick in the entrance, which is accentuated by a wood batten balcony that wraps around the corner. These material combinations and variations are part of Aalto's palette in many other houses; in Kantola, a large house of some fifteen rooms, they soften its somewhat official character.

In plan the interior resembles that of the Aalto House, with rooms gathered around a core space— in Kantola's case a hall on both floors. The two halls connect to the outdoors with a terrace on the ground level and a balcony on the second floor. Just as in the Aalto residence, the public spaces are on the ground floor, as the house often served as a place for official occasions and parties. Nearest to the entrance is the study, which could be used as a home

office. Other main spaces, such as the dining hall and the living room, open onto the garden, while the private spaces, including the bedrooms, guest rooms, and servant quarters are on the second floor.

Upon entering the house, visitors take two turns to arrive at the hall, at whose end a garden and view to the sea open. The importance of the hall is emphasized with a fireplace and a large corner window looking out onto the garden. Two free-standing steel columns wrapped with rattan flank the garden entrance. Outdoor spaces, terraces, and balconies play an important role in Kantola and enrich the simple volume.

In the early 1960s Kantola was altered to serve as the executive staff club. Currently, the house is jointly owned by the Sunila company and the city of Kotka and is used for meetings and guest accommodation.

top
Site plan

bottom
First-floor plan and north and west facades

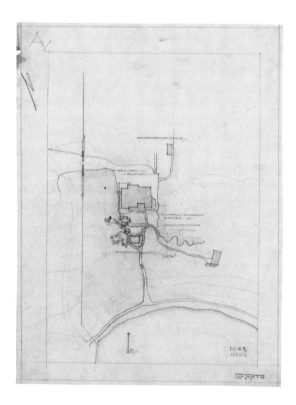

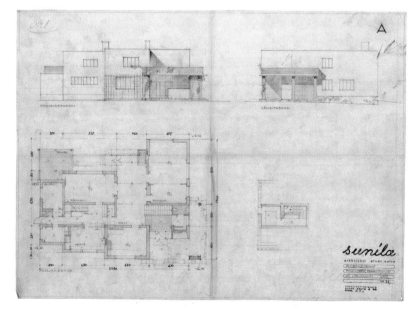

top
Kantola in 1937

bottom
**A view toward the house
over the stonewall**

top
View of the garden-side entrance

bottom
Second-floor hall

opposite
The hall-cum-living room faces the garden and lake. The armchair, Tank, was designed in 1936. On the left is a stackable armchair designed for the Paimio Sanatorium in 1931–32.

Foremen's Houses and
Mäntylä, Senior Engineer's House

Tampella Company
Inkeroinen, Kouvola, Finland
1937

Located some nineteen miles north of Sunila, Inkeroinen by the Kymijoki River has had a history as a wood industry site since the 1870s. The production of the Inkeroinen plant focused on cardboard and ground paper products, and its owner, the Tampella company, was also one of the founders of the Sunila pulp mill. As the Sunila project proved to be successful, Tampella commissioned Aalto in the 1930s and 1940s for various projects in the Kymijoki River area, with the first dating from 1937.[15]

In addition to designing a paper mill, Aalto in the first phase complemented an existing residential area with several types of detached and single-family houses, including five detached foremen's houses and three engineers' houses, as well as a group of wooden workers' row houses.[16] Situated between two industrial blocks, the residential area is marked much more by the traditional hierarchy of the factory community than the Sunila area. Workers', foremen's, and engineers' houses are placed in their respective groups and have distinct architectural characters.

The five semi-detached foremen's houses are sited by the Kymijoki River on a slope facing west. Views from the houses and their gardens are exceptional, with rapids beneath and a forest on the other side of the river, as well as the power station somewhat downstream. In plan, the dwellings in the two-story houses are mirror images, with living and dining rooms on the ground floor, and two bedrooms and a bathroom upstairs. An unusual accent on the exterior is the placement of the chimney on the outer wall, contrary to the traditional position in the middle, resulting in a counterbalance to the otherwise horizontal volume.

The three engineers' houses are located closest to the factory and built on a steep slope, so that they are partly two and partly three stories high. Aalto placed each house based on the topography of the site, so that the buildings are not in a straight line. Open gardens surround them, with no clear borders between the public and private areas.

The architectural character of both the foremen's and engineers' houses is quite surprising for the time they were built. Instead of flat roofs and other modern elements, they feature steep saddleback brick roofs and are more reminiscent of Danish countryside farmhouses than modern factory residencies, with their asymmetrical volumes, terraces, canopies, and dormer windows. The white rendering of the walls is complemented by dark horizontal cladding on the gable ends of the foremen's houses, while in the engineers' houses dark-stained wooden boarding is used as accents in the terraces and entrances. One reason for the surprising difference from the simultaneous Sunila houses could be Tampella's more conservative attitude, which might have affected Aalto's choice of a traditional volume.[17]

opposite
**The curving entrance driveway
to the Foremen's Houses**

76

The residence of the chief engineer, called Mäntylä, is the largest of the engineers' houses group, and its plan layout is repeated in the two smaller houses. Although the room arrangement is typical for Aalto's houses during the 1930s, with the sequence of a hall and adjacent dining room, living room, and study, there is an especially fine spatial and visual continuity through the house. A window in the main staircase provides natural light to the entrance hall, from which views open up through the living and dining room to the tree-tops outside. The main entrance is turned sideways, so that the vestibule feels private and modest.

Both the entrance and the upstairs hall are comfortable with open fireplaces providing places to sit and relax. Mäntylä's spacious atmosphere is reinforced by large windows, especially in the living room, which bring the surrounding nature into the house. In addition, a terrace serves as a continuation of the indoor space, while a balcony above offers views southward and onto the garden. The main first-floor rooms are separated with sliding doors and can be joined into one continuous space, while the kitchen and servants' rooms are separated from the rest of the house, accessible by a side entrance—a sign of the building's inner hierarchy. On the second floor three bedrooms and a guest room are gathered around the hall.

Since the 1990s Mäntylä has been used for corporate purposes.

opposite
A steep slope characterizes the garden side of the foremen's houses.

top
View of the houses from the river

middle left
Foremen's Houses, living room

middle right
Second-floor staircase and hall with dormer window

bottom
First-floor plan

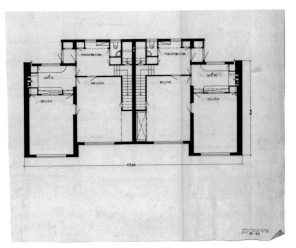

left
**Mäntylä, sketch of the
south facade**

right
Mäntylä, floor plans

opposite
**A view of Mäntylä from
the garden**

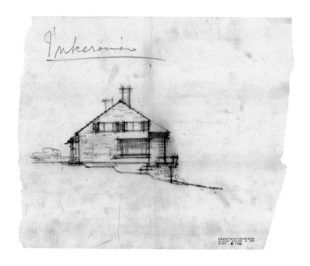

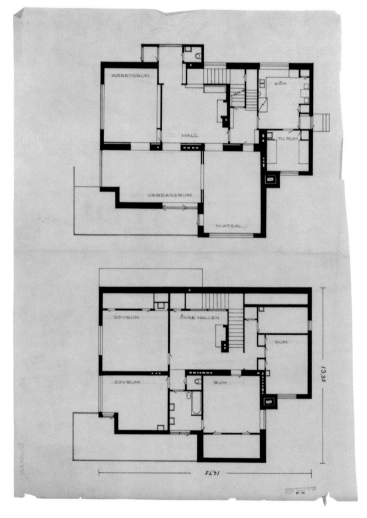

Villa Mairea

Noormarkku, Finland
1938–39

The last house Aino and Alvar Aalto designed in the 1930s ended the decade with a bang. The Villa Mairea in Noormarkku is the most complex and detailed of all of Aalto's private home designs. Commissioned by Harry and Maire Gullichsen, it was born from a close friendship and based on the friends' common thoughts on modern lifestyle. Both Maire Gullichsen's father and grandfather had built houses on the same property in this region of west Finland—the A. Ahlström company's homebase—but the young couple (the Gullichsens were in their early thirties and the Aaltos in their forties) wanted their home to reflect their own radical concepts. As Aalto explained in 1939, the Villa Mairea was to serve as an architectural laboratory as well as a social experiment. The hope was that this kind of luxurious villa would serve as a model for a frame for life that could be made available to all due to the country's increasing welfare:

> All the same, an architectural assignment based on an individual lifestyle, instinct and conception of culture can have far-reaching social significance in the long run.... The individual architectural assignment can be treated as a laboratory experiment of sorts, in which things can be done that would be impossible with present-day mass-production, and those can spread further and eventually become available to one and all as production methods advance.[18]

The process of designing the villa took place in several phases. Early exterior perspective sketches show the influence of Frank Lloyd Wright's Fallingwater (1935) on Aalto, especially in the villa's volumetric composition with horizontal cantilevered balconies. At this early stage the interior had a high hall with free-form elements, a concept Aalto abandoned with the so-called proto-Mairea, which had a separate art gallery volume, while the main rooms of the house were grouped around a staircase. When work on the foundations was already in progress, Aalto changed his plans again and now combined the house's separate formal rooms, including the art gallery, living room, dining room, and hall into one unity—a single large room on the ground floor with various functions and uses. This continuity of spaces with areas separated only by their different characters gave the Villa Mairea's main floor its flow, ambiguity, and, surprisingly, also its coziness. None of the areas is too large, and from each nook one can see the others. As Göran Schildt has pointed out, the flexible living room was an experimental return back to the rural *tupa* and belongs among the folkloristic accents of the house.[19] Aalto described it in 1939 as "a single large living room...for the family's everyday use.... [A] continuous room with partitions that can be grouped freely was designed to form a single architectural entity, in which painting and everyday life can evolve in a more direct manner."[20] An essential factor on this level is also the connection to the

top
**Sketch of the southeast
facade**

bottom
**Villa Mairea in the middle
of pine trees**

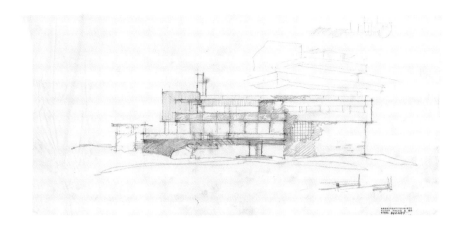

garden with views of the pine tree landscape around the house.

Being surrounded by nature and being at the same time in contrast and in harmony with it is the essence of the Villa Mairea. From a distance, its white flat-roofed modern volume is visible among the vertical rhythm of pine trees. The slightly sloping terrain and a softly curving driveway gradually reveal the villa's warm-hued wooden claddings and details. Wood is wrapped around the most important spaces, including the living room and Maire Gullichsen's atelier. The whiteness of the facades has a soft touch with the visible texture of brickwork underneath.

The image of the forest is carried inside through groups of vertical wooden poles, which give rhythm to the interior and direct the eye and movement. Supporting the canopy, a group of poles guards the entrance, while in the hall another group shields the staircase, accompanying the visitor upstairs, where a view from the window opens up to the trees of the forest, which seem to continue the rhythm.

The inner landscape of the Villa Mairea is unique among Aalto's houses. In his smaller homes, the main rooms are often in groups of three—united but still separate, while in the Villa Mairea the connections between the different parts of the main space seem to have an endless number of variations. There are always two or three different areas of the space in one's sight, often including a view of the outdoor courtyard or natural landscape. This richness is increased by the transparency of the main staircase and the contrasting heaviness of the hearth. The smallest details, from the rattan bindings around the columns to the beautifully finished woodwork, bring the spatial experience to a tactile level. Aino Aalto designed much of the interior and the individual furniture, though standard Artek models were used as well.

A continuous beech ceiling gives a warm tone to the interior and connects the separate library with the main room. Originally, the library partition walls with bookcases were movable. This, together with the sliding glass doors opening to the garden gave the space an atmosphere of momentariness. Due to the need for privacy in the library, though, undulating glass and plywood were later added between the wall cabinets and the ceiling, resulting in permanency and enclosure.

The interior also has many allusions to traditional Japanese architecture, especially in the flower room, whose latticework wall resembles *shoji* (sliding screens) and which features bamboo shelves on the walls, to mention some obvious loans. The presence of Japanese references and details is often explained by Aalto's ability to assimilate many ideas and influences into his process of synthesis. He was clearly inspired by several books on Japanese architecture he received while designing the Villa Mairea and he may have visited a Japanese teahouse in Stockholm. Still, the Villa Mairea remains the only one of his houses where these sensitive touches were materialized.

Art was an inseparable part of the villa, as Maire Gullichsen was an art patron, had studied art, and founded the Free Art School in Helsinki in 1935. She also initiated many modern art exhibitions in Finland and became an art collector. Her studio, covered on the outside with dark-stained wooden battens, is one of the most recognizable parts of the house with its high, smoothly rounded volume that crowns the garden corner. A small staircase—almost hidden—leads from the living room to the double-height atelier, which has an atmosphere of concentration. Its position in the corner of the villa gives it privacy and offers the best possible views onto the courtyard through a large window. The studio's white-painted concrete ceiling beams, tiled floor, and partly wooden-clad walls are the materials of a workroom. Along the rear wall, steep wooden stairs with handrails made of rope lead up to a small interior balcony used for storage.

On the second floor of the main wing are the private rooms located along an extended upper hall, including two master bedrooms and children's bedrooms, whose bay windows form a distinct feature on the front facade. There is also a separate wing for guestrooms.

The Villa Mairea is characterized by its abundance of rich details, including various sheathings around columns, softly curving handrails, and the sculptural forms of the fireplace and the bottom tread of the staircase. The spaces' different rhythms and hues are like the richness of nature with its endless variations brought into architectural forms. Vernacular elements, such as the solid fireplace or the sod roofs of the detached sauna building and the garden patio are intertwined with sculptural abstraction and white modernism. When architect Eero Saarinen (1910–1961) visited the villa in 1958, he particularly admired Aalto's use of wood, which expressed rich imagination and a unique sense of form and material.[21]

The sensitivity continues in the garden courtyard, which is embraced by the building, stonewalls, and a low earth mound, and fuses with the forest at its end, without clear boundaries. A bright turquoise free-form swimming pool with reflecting water contrasts with the dark logs of the sauna building, which is connected to the main house by a sod-roofed patio. A single pine tree grows near the corner of the patio and stretches its branches over the pool, reminiscent of a Japanese *sumi-e* painting.

The uniqueness of the Villa Mairea arises from the remarkable synthesis Aalto has created in its design. The details of the house are like small pearls amid the flow of space and were an integral part of the planning process. The Villa Mairea combines many motifs and elements of Aalto's previous and later buildings, such as the wood-clad exterior of the Aalto House, the rattan-wrapped columns and the stone wall of Kantola, the grass roof of the 1940s cabins and saunas, the free-form canopy of the Paimio Sanatorium, the grouped columns of the Paris Exhibition pavilion, and the key role art plays in the Maison Carré and the Maison Aho.

The house is presently owned by the A. Ahlström company and used for formal occasions. Family members sometimes spend vacation time there, and the house is open to the public by appointment.

top
Site plan

bottom
Maire Gullichsen, Alvar Aalto, and architect Paul Bernoulli at the construction site in 1938

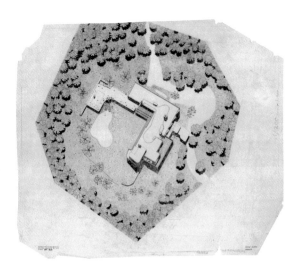

top
First-floor plan

bottom
Second-floor plan

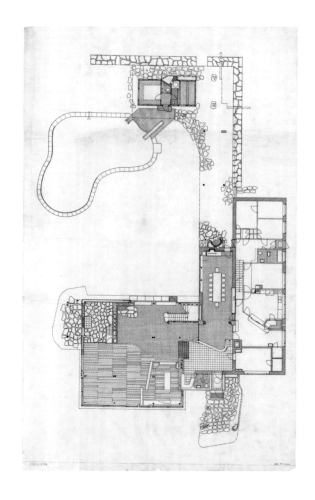

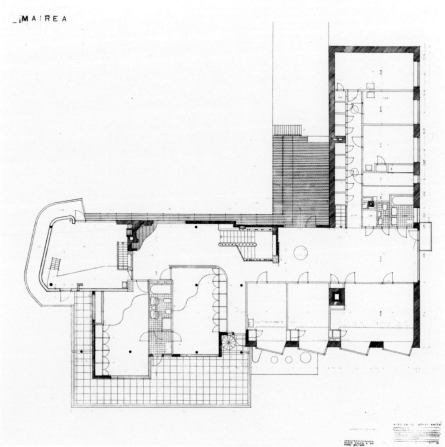

top
**The second-floor bedroom
bay windows with their
refined detailing**

bottom
**View to the service wing
from the northeast**

right
**View of the garden
facades from the pool**

right

Living room. On the
back wall are Massimo
Campigli's *Ritratto di
Signora* (1931), left, and
The Yellow Guitar by
Juan Gris (1926), right.
In the foreground is the
Safari chair, designed by
Maija Heikinheimo for
Artek in 1960.

below
The entrance hall with a view
toward the living room greets
visitors with forest motifs
and art displays. The art works
in the hall include Alexander
Calder's mobile from 1940
and two lithographs by Pablo
Picasso from 1947. The blue
bench was designed by Aino
Aalto in 1939.

opposite
The staircase leading to
the second floor from the
living room plays an iconic
role in the forest landscape
of the villa.

left
Maire Gullichsen's atelier on
the second floor. The floor
lamp was designed by Aino
Aalto in the 1930s. The bust of
Maire Gullichsen in the
background is by Gunnar
Elfgren (1935).

right
Flower room with bamboo
shelves and rattan furniture

below
The music space in the living
room features a grand piano
by Poul Henningsen (1936).
The painting on the left is
Serge Poliakoff's *Composition
Abstraite* (1954). The marble
sculpture, *Torso de Ange*
(1963), is by Jean Arp.

below

The library features a black
armchair by Aino Aalto in
front and floor lamps by
Viljo Hirvonen for Artek (1953).
Hirvonen's company
Valaistustyö fabricated all
Aalto lamps during 1953–75.

The 1940s: Standard Houses and Summer Cottages

With the start of World War Two in 1939, political tensions broke out throughout Europe. Finland's first military conflict with the Soviet Union, the Winter War of 1939 to 1940, was soon followed by the Continuation War (1941–44). The decade was thus dominated by destruction and subsequent reconstruction. Over four hundred thousand inhabitants of Finnish Karelia and other ceded territories had to be evacuated and resettled into other parts of the country. As all evacuees and war veterans were given the right to receive a homestead, this resulted in an acute and massive need for quick and cheap housing. Material shortages and building regulations made this task especially challenging and continued to restrict the construction industry in Finland until the 1950s. Wooden buildings and simple structures were a common solution to the problem.

Aalto's main role in the early 1940s was to initiate and organize the work of the Reconstruction Office of the Finnish Association of Architects. He also gave war propaganda and reconstruction lectures in Sweden, Switzerland, and the United States, where he held a professorship at the Massachusetts Institute of Technology since 1940. In 1943 he was elected chairman of the Finnish Association of Architects, a position he held for the next fifteen years.

Projects in Aalto's office ranged from small-scale industrial buildings and reconstruction tasks to regional planning and master plans. Commissions for large public buildings began to emerge at the end of the decade. While standardized housing was an important element of Aalto's work in the early 1940s, he strongly advocated for a humane approach, stating in 1941:

> We must also understand that a building cannot fulfill its purpose if it does not itself possess a wealth of nuances equal to that of the natural environment to which it will belong as a permanent ingredient....
> In the name of common sense, any standardization that can come into consideration here must be of the decentralizing type. The purpose of architectural standardization is thus not to produce types, but instead to create variety and richness which could, in the ideal case, be compared with nature's unlimited capacity to produce variation.[1]

opposite
Site Manager's House, A. Ahlström Company (VOK Standard House)

Asevelikylä, Housing for Ex-service Men (Standard Houses)

Nekala, Tampere, Finland
1940–41

Aalto had been designing standardized house types since the late 1930s, based on an initiative of the A. Ahlström company, which in 1937 started serial production of Aalto's wooden houses, first at their sawmill, and from 1940 onwards at the Varkaus housing factory, with the goal to build inexpensive, but modern one-family houses. The first types had only a few factory-made parts, such as windows and doors, but were built of measured and ready-cut sawn wood. Typical architectural features included asymmetrical rooflines with long verandas. These standardized houses were mainly built in locations where there was an A. Ahlström production plant.

In the 1940s the AA-system followed, a selection of wooden housing components with a wide range of internal variables, which complied better with Aalto's vision of flexible standard-ization.[2] He would use the AA-system for a variety of standard houses based on the different needs of clients and site conditions. Among Aalto's early type-planned houses was the Asevelikylä area in Tampere, a city in south Finland, which provided housing for ex-service men.

Immediately after the Winter War in 1940, the Finnish state passed a law that facilitated the resettlement of people from the ceded regions and war veterans. In Tampere the housing shortage was especially severe, and the Brother-in-Arms

Association of the city's Nekala neighborhood started a fund-raising campaign in 1940 to help families whose fathers had fallen or who otherwise lived in bad conditions. The association rented land for this project of twenty-six houses from the city of Tampere and commissioned drawings from Aalto, based on his AA-system. The Varkaus factory produced the wooden parts for the type-planned houses, and in May 1941 hundreds of people helped dig the grounds and build the houses.[3] Up to two hundred volunteers worked on the site every evening, forming an essential resource for building up the area. The Continuation War interrupted the project but did not prevent volunteers and paid workers to continue their efforts. In December 1942 the first semi-detached house was ready to house two families, and in September 1943, Risto Ryti (1889–1956), then president of Finland, held a speech to inaugurate the village.[4]

Thirteen semi-detached houses were eventually built in Nekala, each with its own garden plot—a vital requirement for growing food and enabling self-sufficiency during the rationing years. The houses had symmetrical plans of two small apartments each, with two rooms and a kitchenette as well as some storage space in the basement. The area also included a communal sauna and laundry house.[5] Aalto created variation within the simple plan in an interesting way by

arranging the living rooms of the two apartments differently; in one apartment, space for a terrace was cut from the living room, while in the other a bay window extends the living room on the diagonal and opens a view to the garden. He also varied the design with the individual treatment of porches and terraces with nooks and canopies. The tiny kitchenettes of the Nekala homes were unusual for the time, as other type-planned war veteran houses provided much larger kitchens with enough space to fit a dining table.

An article in the Finnish magazine *Kotiliesi* from 1943 speaks about everyday practical issues in the brandnew homes. The sizes of the families living at Nekala varied from three to eleven people, and the most challenging task for these families was to find sleeping spaces for all family members in the small apartments. The modern kitchen equipment and facilities were appreciated but some criticism was given to the size of the kitchen and the lack of a dining corner:

> When approaching the houses they seem to be ordinary countryside dwellings, but a closer look reveals details such as the tarred, raking columns in the porches and the sharp-cornered window protruding from the facade.... When we visited a charming family of six, they told us how they had enjoyed moving here from a cramped city home with only one room and a shared kitchen. Here all four children can grow up close to nature.... In a small home like this with the mother burdened by housework, it would be preferable if breakfast could be served at the kitchen table. It would save legwork, and especially in the mornings the kitchen is the only ventilated room.... It might be possible to design a family dining corner in our small apartments, like the Americans have.[6]

The asymmetrical roof lines and horizontal boarding and windows give the Nekala houses a modern appearance, while round tarred timbers were used for the porch structure, railings, and ladders. The raking columns supporting the porch roof repeated the detailing Aalto had used in the Villa Mairea and which would be typical for him in other 1940s buildings. Entrances to the two apartments were on opposite ends of each house and the terraces were oriented to different directions, thus providing privacy for the inhabitants. To this day Nekala is a verdant and pleasant residential area.

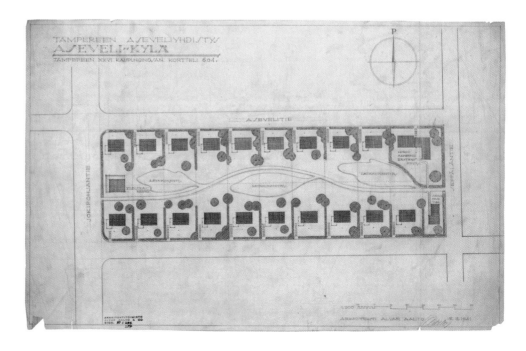

opposite
Original plan of the area with
a path and adjacent leaf-
shaped playgrounds in the
middle of the block.

top
The village was inaugurated
in 1943.

bottom
Plans, facades, and section

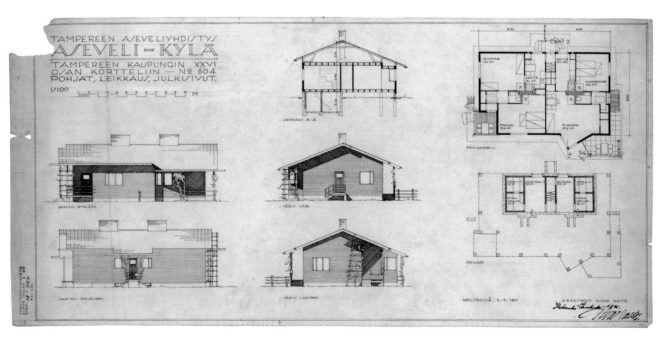

top
Living room detail

bottom
View from the front garden

opposite
Living room

Site Manager's House (VOK Standard Houses)

A. Ahlström Company
Pihlava, Pori, Finland
1946

Another house type Aalto developed based on the AA-system was the Varkaus standard house (single-family home, known as VOK). Compared with his other type-plan houses, the VOK houses were more spacious and meant for officials. Designed in 1941, they would be built during the next decade in various industrial areas where the A. Ahlström company had its factories. In Pihlava in west Finland, where the company operated a large sawmill, which in the late 1940s was extended with a fiberboard factory, Aalto designed a house for the site manager based on VOK standard drawings in 1946.[7]

The plan of the site manager's house is very compact, almost square. Only the entrance areas are marked with a recess, terraces, and canopies. A large, brick hipped roof with long eaves covers the building and acts almost like a fourth facade. The exterior image with its extended horizontal lines is reminiscent of Frank Lloyd Wright's single-family house architecture. Various types of wooden cladding—on the lower part of the facade latticework covers the horizontal weatherboarding, while around the entrance narrow vertical lathing is used—and details give the house a refined touch. The building is rooted in place through a terrace wall of natural stone. From the terrace a view over a small artificial pond opens, and from here a stone-paved path leads to the garden, designed by landscape architect Paul Olsson.[8]

Despite the compact volume, Aalto managed to create a sense of spatial continuum through the diagonally connected main rooms. The living and dining spaces form a whole that opens immediately upon entering the house. The rooms were given a warm atmosphere through the use of wooden walls and ceilings. Private spaces, including bedrooms and a kitchen, occupy the other half of the house along an L-shaped row. Today the building is privately owned.

opposite
View toward the house across a small pond

VIRKAMIE/A/UNTO/

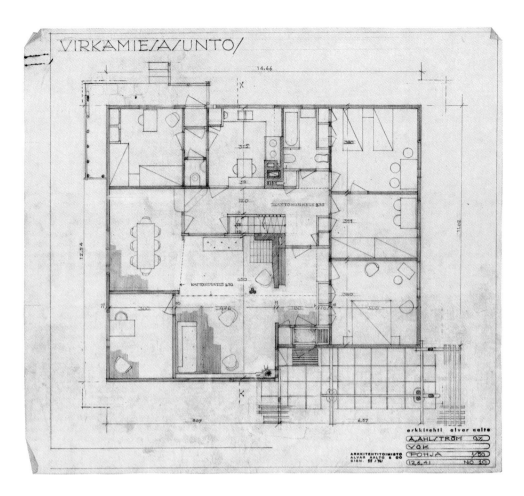

arkkitehti alvar aalto

A,AHL/TRÖM OY
VOK
POHJA 1/50
12,6,41 NO 10

ARKKITEHTITOIMISTO
ALVAR AALTO & OO
SIGN. 89 /761

VIRKAMIE/A/UNTO/

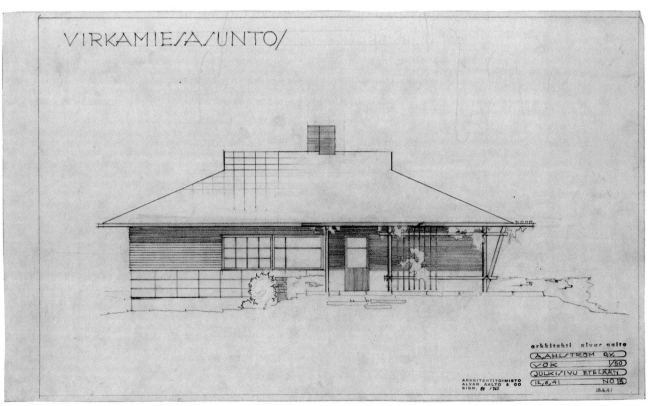

arkkitehti alvar aalto

A,AHL/TRÖM OY
VOK
JULKI/IVU ETELÄÄN 1/50
12,6,41 NO 13

ARKKITEHTITOIMISTO
ALVAR AALTO & OO
SIGN. 89 /765

18.6.41

opposite top
Floor plan

opposite bottom
South facade

below
**The living room and terrace
open onto the garden.**

below
The terrace entrance was
made of slate and wood,
materials that were typical for
the time.

opposite
The living room corner
features an open fireplace
and armchairs designed by
Aalto in 1947.

Manager's House

Yhteissisu Company
Vanaja, Hämeenlinna, Finland
1945–46

The Yhteissisu company was founded in 1943 to respond to the urgent need for vehicles, trucks, and buses for the Finnish army and civilians during the war years. The wide ownership included the state of Finland and various industrial corporations, among which were the A. Ahlström company, the Kone company, the Tampella company, and United Paper Mills. Yhteissisu requested a master plan from Aalto in the summer of 1944 and approved the plan early the following year. In addition to a house for the company's manager, Aalto designed other staff housing, including three row houses, eight single-family houses, and an apartment building, although his master plan for the area was not fully carried out.[9]

The manager's house combines the character of late 1930s and early 1940s standardized houses with the individuality of the Villa Mairea. Located apart from other staff dwellings, the site for the residence is wooded and descends steeply southward. The sloping site gave rise to natural stonewall structures that form terraces in front of the house and line a wide porch on the southern and western side of the building. The inclined basement wall is lined with slate, part of the typical 1940s material palette together with the brick roof. The official character of the house is expressed in the use of wooden columns to support the porch and pergola. As in other Aalto buildings of this decade, they are rhythmically grouped and raked when in a corner position.

The first-floor plan features the architect's familiar three-room sequence, accessed from the hall: the living room, dining room, and study, which all share a view to the garden. The hall serves as an intermediate space, with a brick floor emphasizing its outdoor role. While it is a few steps above the level of the main rooms, it is spatially fully integrated with the living room through the use of a plywood board ceiling that continues without interruption, as well as through brick steps leading down to the living room. The main staircase is another intermediate element, forming part of the interior landscape of the living area and at the same time hiding the kitchen, pantry, and servants' room behind it. The partly freestanding element with its wooden latticework is further accentuated by adjacent rope-covered double columns and an integrated fireplace built on an extension of the brick steps. The combination of staircase and fireplace is a familiar theme that Aalto also used in the studio wing of his own house. Nods to the Villa Mairea are obvious in the stonewalls, column details, and in the position and detailing of the staircase.

opposite
View of the house from the garden with its stone terraces and walls

top
South facade

bottom
Detail drawings for the staircase and open fireplace

opposite
View of the approach

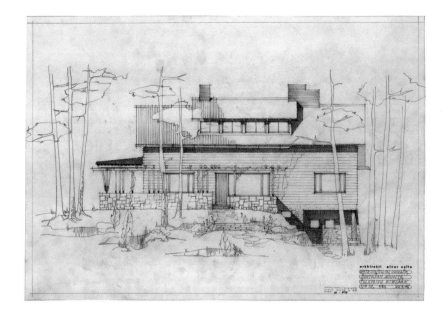

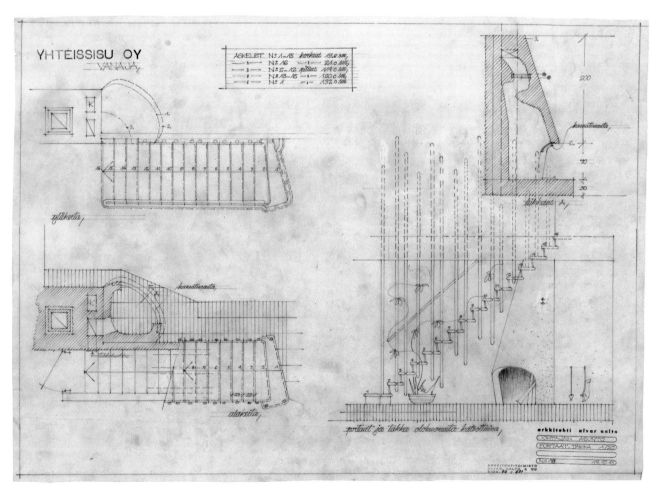

below
**View from the living room
toward the hall and staircase**

opposite
**Study. Aalto designed the
Flying Saucer ceiling light for
the National Pensions Institute
in the 1950s. The glass top
table with Y-shaped legs is
from 1947.**

Korpikoto Hunting Lodge

Pertunmaa, Finland

1945

Small-scale commissions became more important for Aalto's office in the 1940s, because of the general difficulties the construction industry faced during the war and the subsequent period of rebuilding, and the temporary lack of larger projects. Two of these smaller commissions consisted of private summer houses designed for managers of a major industrial client, the Tampella company: Major Jörgen Schauman, who was the works manager at the Tampella factory in Inkeroinen, commissioned the Korpikoto Hunting Lodge in 1945, and Åke Kihlman, a Tampella director, later managing director and a widely influential person in the Finnish postwar industrial field, asked Aalto to design a summer residence, the Villa Kihlman, in 1947.

Jörgen Schauman took great interest in hunting, and his small cabin, located in the lake district of south Finland, could serve as a base for autumn bird hunting. Originally consisting of a single room with a sauna, the Korpikoto Lodge's appearance has elements of Finnish and German vernacular architecture combined with features reminiscent of wartime front line dugouts, the latter including the roughly worked wooden structure and details such as wooden gutters.[10] The building's horizontal cladding, wooden window shutters, decorative wrought iron hinges, and its turf roof emphasize its rustic character, as do two spruce logs that support a heavy round beam in the porch canopy. The atmosphere is perfectly in balance with the cabin's use: to rest in its warmth after a hunt.

opposite
View of the lodge from the lakeside

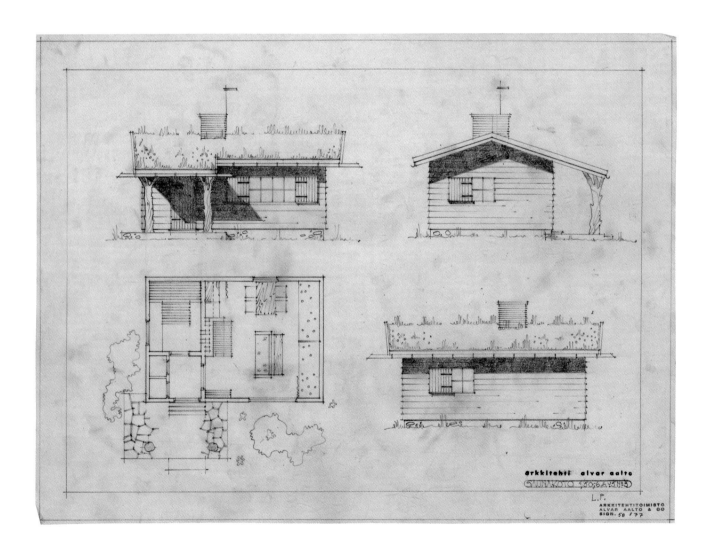

below
**Open fireplace in the
main room**

opposite
Main room

Villa Kihlman

Kuru, Ylöjärvi, Finland
1947–48

Villa Kihlman is a one-story summer home that shares features with the Korpikoto Hunting Lodge, such as the small-paned windows with shutters and dark brown exterior walls. The villa's log walls with long ends, left exposed on the interior, represent Finnish tradition at its purest. In the late 1940s, Aalto designed several log buildings that are generally considered part of his Karelian period. The architect was clearly inspired by Karelian vernacular houses, but another reason for using logs could have been the shortage of building materials during the 1940s.

The villa's location in the backwoods makes it a perfect place for retreat. A stonewall outlines the terrace, which is a few steps above the terrain level. The plan shows a clear division of spatial hierarchy, with a large living room that has views in three directions and a big fireplace-stove, and four private bedrooms that are grouped together. The modern kitchen with cabinets designed by Aino Aalto and an adjacent servant's room has its own entrance. The exposed logs of the small entrance hall and living room give the interior an archaic character.

opposite
The Villa Kihlman is characterized by exposed log walls and wooden window shutters.

top
Main facade

bottom
Floor plan

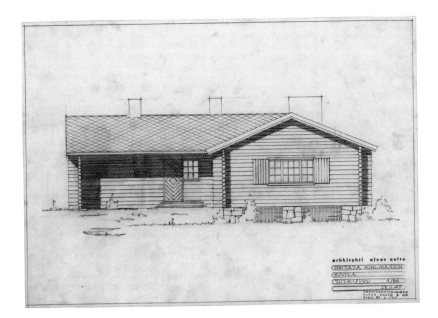

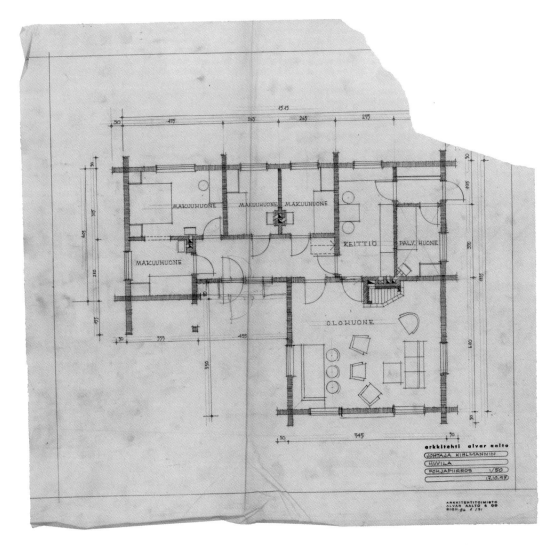

top
**View of the house from
the lake**

bottom
**A stone wall encloses
the entrance terrace.**

Villa Manner

Sondby, Porvoo, Finland
1951–52

Villa Manner was built on a seashore plot in south
Finland for Aalto's second cousin Eero Manner,
a justice of the Supreme Court. In this summer house
Aalto returns to the loggia theme of his earlier work,
but here the porch with its round, wooden columns
is joined to a modern building with panorama
windows. The half-open terrace serves as an outdoor
living and dining space during summer days and
evenings. The character of the villa's wooden
structures and details is reminiscent of earlier Aalto
houses but also precedes future features. Especially
the living room wall paneling and the exposed
ceiling beams were elements that the architect
would use in later projects in different variations.
The combination of the wooden panels and white-
painted wall surface is at the same time warm
and light.

opposite
**View of the terrace
colonnade in fall**

top
Floor plan

bottom
Sketch for the seaside facade

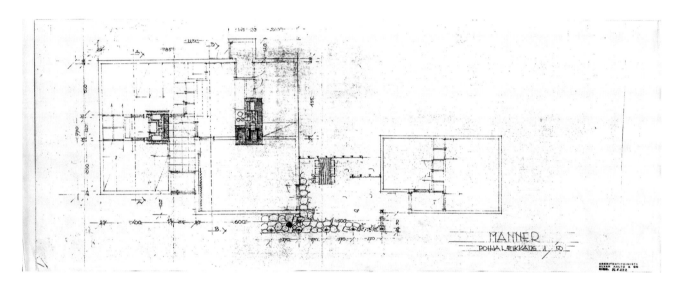

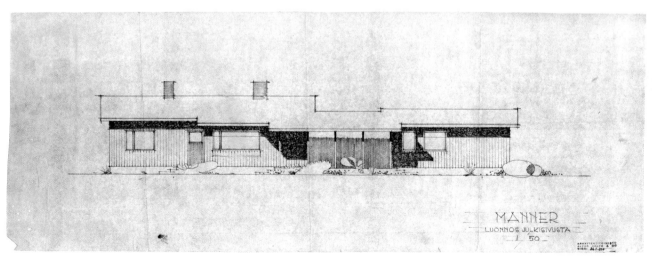

below
**Living room. Aalto exhibited a
model of the armchair at the
Milan Triennial in 1933.**

opposite
**The sheltered terrace
functions as a second living
room during the summer
months.**

The 1950s: Experiments and Refinement

Finland began building a welfare state in the 1950s, and although the country was still struggling to make war payments at the beginning of the decade, reconstruction efforts were underway and there was a prevailing sense of optimism. The 1952 Olympic Summer Games held in Helsinki symbolized both the country's internationalization and postwar recovery. Industrial growth, urbanization, and an increasing need for new buildings to accommodate education and administration purposes were all part of Finland's modernization.

Although Aalto still worked on a fair amount of industrial commissions, he increasingly received large public projects, such as the university campuses in Jyväskylä (1951–71) and Otaniemi, Espoo (1949–74), the Helsinki House of Culture (1952–58), and Kansaneläkelaitos (National Pensions Institution) office building (Helsinki, 1950–57), as well as other office and cultural buildings, which soon began to take up the majority of his office's work. Many of the architect's most outstanding designs fall into this decade. His mature architecture continued to explore his favorite themes and motifs but in a more complex way, and his 1950s houses are often multifaceted compositions in the landscape with interiors that feature variations of indoor-outdoor spaces. Red brick, together with copper and natural stone, became Aalto's favorite materials for their durability and graceful aging.

opposite
**Muuratsalo
Experimental House,
detail of atrium
courtyard facade**

Muuratsalo Experimental House

Säynätsalo, Jyväskylä, Finland
1952–53

Aalto's personal life in the 1950s was shaped by the tragedy of Aino Aalto's death in 1949 and his marriage to Elsa (Elissa) Mäkiniemi in 1952. The Muuratsalo Experimental House symbolizes the new start for the couple, who found the site for their summer residence on Muuratsalo Island in Lake Päijänne during the construction phase of the Säynätsalo Town Hall (1949–52), located nearby. The central Finnish landscape with its hills and lakes was one of Aalto's favorite regions.

The position of the summer house seems to be determined by the rock outcrop of the cove in which it sits, providing a panoramic view of the lake, but as you approach it, the house shows its many different faces, which act as extensions of the site's various landscapes. The view from the lake resembles an acropolis, with the house representing an imposing white temple rising from the bedrock. As you come closer, the building acts as a gateway next to the rising rock that guards it. From the forest side, the image changes to that of a winding path with several small structures at the foot of the hill. From the back, the summer residence appears like a sheltering wall in the forest, while its atrium courtyard on the other side, an intermediary element between inside and out, invites the visitor in.

The courtyard, functioning like an outdoor hall, is the heart of the house. It is monumental and, at the same time, intimate, with an open fireplace at its center that draws guests and residents together on summer evenings. Famous for its brick collages on the facades and floor, the yard served as a testing ground for the durability of various ceramic materials and their appearance. For this Aalto ordered bricks from several manufacturers, as his goal was to try out all types that were available at the time. During the mid-1950s, he attempted to convince the Finnish tax office to approve expenses for the house as experiments in building technology—without success.[1] The architect's testing ground also included the guestroom wing and woodshed, which have different types of foundations. In the detached smoke sauna built about a year after the house was completed, Aalto experimented with the natural tapering shape of logs to form the roof angle. The area around the house was designed by landscape architect Paul Olsson, who had only a few shrubs and bushes planted close to the building, as well as some flowers and climbing vines in the courtyard.

The L-shaped volume of the house is divided into a bedroom wing and a multiuse dining-living-working space with a slanted ceiling. The kitchen

opposite
**The inviting light of the house
in the summer dusk**

faces the forest. The spacious interior of the living room is articulated with exposed ceiling beams and a wooden loft atelier. Most of the walls are finished in a thin-coat rendered brick that echoes the treatment of the exterior. A softer material, insulating fiberboard, was used on the back wall to improve acoustics.

Still to this day numerous details of the highly personal design express how Aalto spent time at the cottage: he liked to paint, swim, enjoy the sauna, and relax—Muuratsalo was his beloved retreat, a place where he could silently listen to nature. His close friend, architect and professor Nils Erik Wickberg, remembers:

When I visited Aalto's new summerhouse in Muuratsalo in 1953, Aalto took me on a hike into the forest and showed me all the rare plants he "had" on his site. And, later, when we sat by the open fire in his yard, he pointed up toward the southern sky where the stars were already shining and said: "And the North Star seems to be there, too."[2]

The Muuratsalo Experimental House is now owned by the Alvar Aalto Foundation and is open to the public during most of the summer months. The Aalto family also continues to use the house as a summer home.

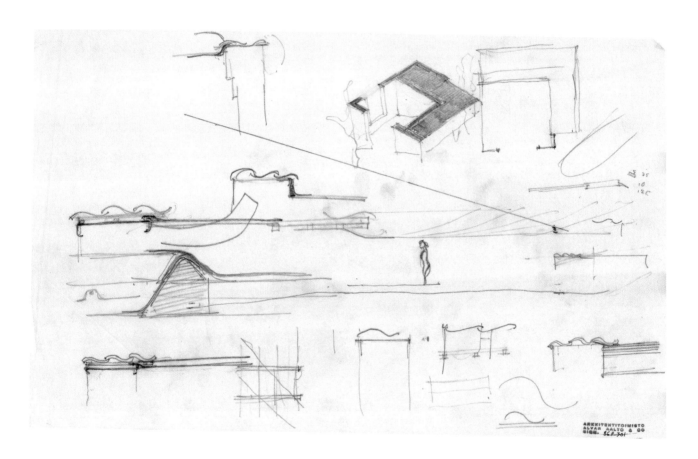

opposite
**Sketches for the atrium
courtyard**

top
**Section through the atrium
courtyard**

middle
Maps of the area

bottom
Site and floor plan

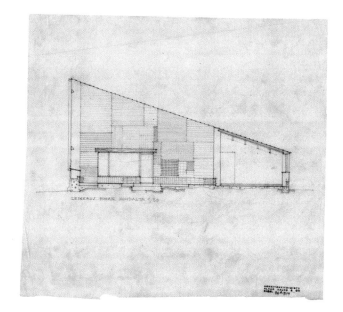

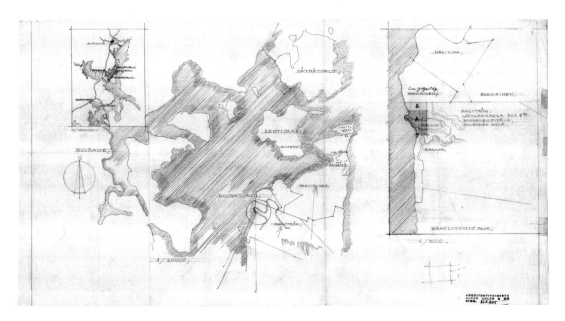

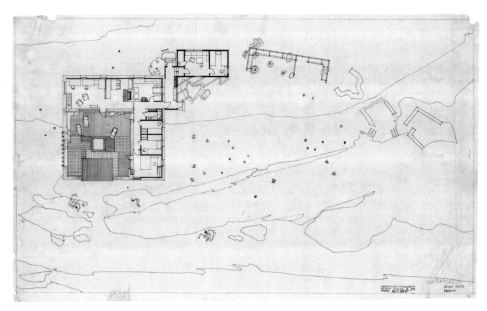

top
**A view of the house
from the forest**

bottom
West facade

top
Aalto painting in the courtyard, 1960s

bottom
Atrium courtyard

opposite

View of the dining corner in the living room. The tablecloth, Pisa, was designed by Elissa Aalto in the 1950s, and the wicker chairs by Maija Heikinheimo for Artek in 1940.

left

Entrance to the kitchen and guest room wing

right

Aalto designed the table lamp in the living room in 1929. Behind the drawing tables on the wall are his sketches of the motor boat *Nemo Propheta in Patria*, which was an important part of life at the summer residence for him.

left
Sauna changing room

right
**The sauna stove is heated
from the outside.**

opposite
**The smoke sauna with its
log walls**

Villa Lehmus, Site Manager's House

Typpi Company
Oulu, Finland
1955–56

Commissions by industrial companies continued in the 1950s, as the pace of industrialization was rapidly accelerating during the postwar years. The wood and paper industries were still dominant, but other fields of industry were growing as well. One goal of the Finnish state was to ensure the self-sufficient production of food supplies, and in connection with this goal the state-owned Typpi company founded a nitrogen fertilizer factory in 1950, located in Oulu in order to support the industrialization program in north Finland. Aalto drew the master plan for the new factory and designed the area's first industrial and residential buildings, the latter situated near the Oulujoki River.

Villa Lehmus was named after the company's first manager, engineer Jaakko Lehmus, who was a pioneer of the Finnish nitrogen industry. Located on a verdant site very close to the riverbank, the two-story building is a compact, squarish volume flanked by a detached one-story sauna and garage wing. The exterior is clad in red brick and articulated by a white-painted canopy above the entrance and multiple balcony structures. Its most conspicuous element is the lean-to roof, which terminates in a concave recess on the garden side. Variations of such free-from rooflines were typical for Aalto in the 1950s.

A letter from Aalto's office to Lehmus describes the essence of the villa's interior:

> The aim has been to create a spatial whole of rooms: a hall, a living room, a dining room, to fit the beautiful surroundings. From the hall the circulation diagonally reaches the dining room and divides the living room into two: a sofa group by the window and a more intimate corner by the fireplace that architecturally dominates the room. The main staircase leading upstairs opens to an upper hall in which there is a hobby corner and a fireplace.[3]

Most of the first floor was occupied with the more formal spaces, including the site manager's office, located closest to the entrance. Spatial flow and openness tie the main rooms together, with views and connections continuing from the living room to the terrace and from the dining room to the serving pantry through a glass cabinet, while wooden latticework creates semi-transparent screens for the staircase and fireplace corner. The functional and spatial arrangement of the living and dining rooms and especially the upstairs bedrooms, hall, and terrace of Villa Lehmus is reminiscent of the Aalto House. This similarity is also seen in other elements of the interior such as the latticework screens and the dining room cabinet.

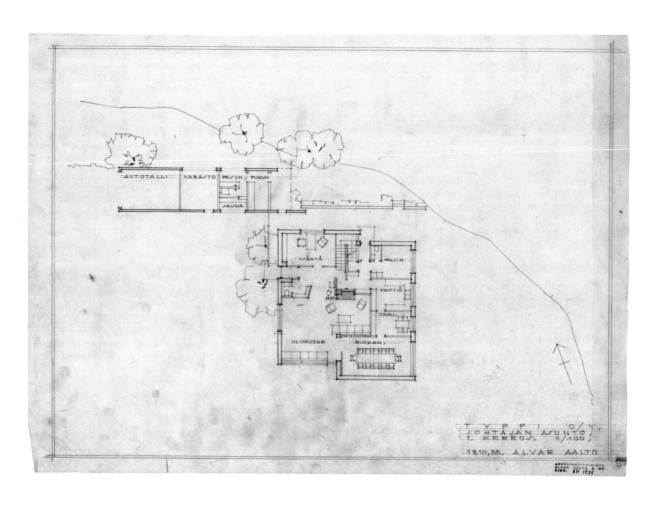

AUTOTALLI VARASTO PESUH. PUKUH.

SAUNA

MÄNTÄ

PALV. H.

KEITTIO

TARJ.

OLOHUONE RUOKAH.

TYPPI O/Y
JOHTAJAN ASUNTO,
1. KERROS, 1/100

19.10.55, ALVAR AALTO

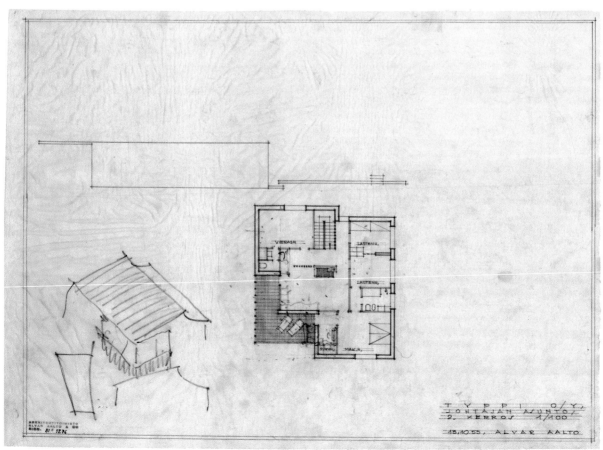

VIERASH.

LASTENH.

LASTENH.

PUKUH. MAK.H.

TYPPI O/Y
JOHTAJAN ASUNTO,
2. KERROS, 1/100

15.10.55, ALVAR AALTO

opposite top
First-floor plan

opposite bottom
Second-floor plan

left
**The concave shape of the
lean-to roof**

right
Second-floor balcony

bottom
View of the approach

left

In the staircase is a Beehive
pendant lamp, designed in
1953. The shelves on the back
wall are Ron Arad's Book
Worm, designed in 1994.

right

The table with socket legs in
the dining room was designed
for the National Pensions
Institute Head Office in 1956.
Many elements of Aalto's
furniture were standards
that he reused in different
combinations.

opposite

View from the entrance
hall to the living room
and terrace

Maison Carré

Bazoches-sur-Guyonne, France
1956–59

Maison Carré is a private house which is to a major extent stamped by the owner being an art collector: one could say that it is at the same time a private "palais" and a gallery. In accordance with the wishes of the owner, the main principle is that family life and art are not separated one from the other; the tendency is the reverse, a very intimate connection between them both.[4]

The above excerpt could be describing the Villa Mairea, but in fact it is how Aalto presented the Maison Carré in *Arkkitehti,* a Finnish architectural journal, in 1961. A series of coincidences had brought the French gallerist and art collector Louis Carré and the Finnish architect together. Carré first opened his Paris gallery in the late 1930s, which would become increasingly notable with exhibitions of Henri Matisse, Raoul Dufy, Fernand Léger, Alexander Calder, and Pablo Picasso during and after World War Two.[5] In the early 1950s, when the art collector decided to build a modern home in the countryside west of Paris, he discussed the question of the future architect with Léger and Calder, who both knew Aalto and recommended him. A Swedish art dealer friend gave Carré the same advice, so he contacted the architect in 1955. The project finally started a year later, after the two had met in Venice and found "a mutual understanding beginning at the diner at Hotel Danieli—with a view on the Grand Canal."[6]

Carré had very specific ideas for his house as he remembers in an interview with author Irmelin Lebeer:

Le Corbusier influenced me greatly, but I was a little apprehensive of his slightly crude, "cement" side.... Especially a house with a roof: I wanted a roof, I don't know why, but I absolutely wanted a roof.... I had several minor requirements: a room surrounded by books, for example, because I need to live with books. And above all, I didn't want anything luxurious.... Above all I had told Aalto: I want a house where I can work.... Also I told Aalto that I wanted a house built with materials that have lived."[7]

Aalto realized his client's wishes in his design for the Maison Carré, which is made of local stone from Chartres, lime-washed bricks, copper, and wood, and features a sloped roof made of slate. The first view that meets the visitor from the winding driveway is the slanting line of the roof, whose imaginary continuation descends along the slightly sloping site and originally extended to the horizon in the open landscape. Since the completion of the house, the trees on the site have grown and the view has been obscured. In the Maison Carré, horizontal and vertical lines are a main compositional element, articulating its volume and exterior facades with

opposite
A curving driveway leads to the house.

precision. The horizontality of the main entrance canopy is emphasized with tapering eaves, while elegant pillars with carpel-like wood articulation serve as a counterbalance. Copper sheeting accentuates the border between the whitewashed brick and travertine stone used for the walls. The dynamic main entrance facade facing north is dominated by the triangle-shaped roofline, while the stepped rectangles of the east elevation interact with the volumes of the low protruding wings on the southern garden side. Terraced stairs descending from the house toward the swimming pool form a podium from which the building rises. In the Maison Carré, Aalto has perhaps created the strongest union of house and landscape. A similar monumentality exists only in the siting of the Muuratsalo Experimental House. In both, there is also a strong touch of Mediterranean culture.

The interior spaces have the same elegant quality as the exterior. Both the Maison Carré and the Villa Mairea are distinguished by their abundance of rich details and variety of materials, although each has a distinct character. The young architect of the Villa Mairea showed rich imagination and passion, which in the Maison Carré has grown into a mature and unified vision. Here also many pieces of the furniture, lamps, and fittings were custom-made for the house, and Elissa Aalto designed many of the textiles.

The main entrance hall is an inner landscape of the highest refinement, with a free-form vaulted ceiling of Finnish red pine, which covers the space like a cupola and draws the visitor into the living room.[8] The wide steps between the hall and the living room accompany the downward movement, which visually continues toward the landscape outdoors. The hall doubles as an art gallery, with paintings hung on the low partition walls. Its role as the heart of the house is again evident, as from it all public spaces can be reached. The transverse living room forms the final point of the meandering diagonal view that starts from the entrance. At its heart is a fireplace, situated opposite a horizontal panoramic window. Paintings by Raoul Dufy, Fernand Léger, and Paul Klee were an inseparable part of the interior, as Louis and Olga Carré specifically chose artworks for the house.[9]

The library Carré had requested repeats at a miniature scale the book pit space Aalto had developed for the Vyborg Library (1927–35), where the interior is divided into different levels to offer quiet, almost enclosed reading spaces. In the Maison Carré's small library the bookcase similarly divides the room into two parts. Also on the ground floor are the master bedrooms and a guestroom, which were given privacy through their placement behind the partition walls. Each room offers direct access to the garden through attached private bathrooms. The second floor was occupied by servants' rooms.

After Louis Carré passed away in 1977, his wife, Olga, lived in the house until 2002. The Finnish Cultural Foundation bought the building in 2006 and donated it to the Association Alvar Aalto en France. The Maison Carré is regularly open to the public.

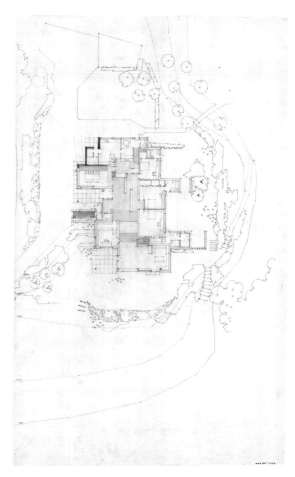

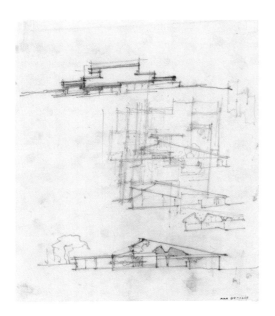

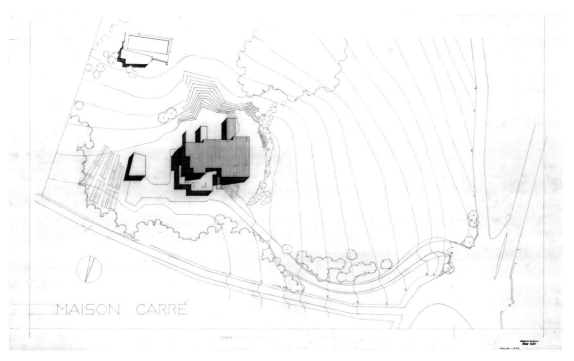

MAISON CARRÉ

opposite

The exhibited art works in the entrance hall included a sculpture by Henri Laurens (*La Grande Sirène*, 1945). The design of the ceiling lamps is similar to the lamps Aalto developed for the Vuoksenniska Church in 1958.

below

The furniture in the foreground of the living room and the Bilberry spot lamps were designed for the Maison Carré. The tapestry is by Harry Kivijärvi (*Theme V*, 1976).

opposite
The asymmetrical lamps
above the dining room table
were designed to provide
light for both the table and
the paintings on the wall.
The Aalto Flower series of
glass vases were developed in
1939 by Aino and Alvar Aalto
for the New York World's
Fair. The sculpture, *Head,*
in the background, from
Harry Kivijärvi's collection,
is a Nigerian bronze work
dating from the thirteenth to
fifteenth centuries.

below
Library

below

**The Turnip pendant lamp in
Louis Carré's bedroom was
designed for the cafe of the
Rautatalo office building in
Helsinki in 1954.**

opposite

**Louis Carré's bathroom
and sauna**

Semi-detached Houses, Site Engineer's House, and Site Manager's House

Enso-Gutzeit Company
Summa, Hamina, Finland
1958–60, 1959–60, 1959–64

The Enso-Gutzeit company, where one of Aalto's former schoolmates, William Lehtinen, had been general manager since 1945, was a new important corporate client for Aalto in the 1950s.[10] Lehtinen had started a vigorous building project to replace the factories that had become part of the Soviet Union after the peace treaty of 1945. As part of this endeavor he commissioned Aalto to draft a master plan for a newspaper factory in Summa in southeast Finland in the mid-1950s. The architect designed both the industrial buildings and a residential area, which was located in a hilly pine forest landscape a short distance from the factory. The area's semi-detached and single-family houses reflect the hierarchy among the factory's employees through the building materials used in each: brick for the engineers and the site manager, and wood for other employees.

The one-story semi-detached houses are placed in straight rows of three and six. The simple volumes with pitched roofs are connected to each other by brown vertical wall cladding that continues as a fence, visible from the street as a rhythmic pattern. As typical for Aalto, the houses turn their backs to the street with enclosed walls or almost unnoticeable entrances, while the main rooms open onto the garden.

The houses for the upper-level staff are sited on a western slope accessed by a small winding road, resembling the 1930s engineers' houses in Inkeroinen, although the 1950s houses have a higher level of integration with their surroundings. Aalto clearly designed the group with the landscape and the surrounding forest in mind and as inspiration. The buildings seem to blend with the rocks and pine trees: their varied and graded volumes follow the shapes of the terrain, while their materials and colors merge with the changing vegetation throughout the seasons. The exterior material palette brings together the lightness of modernism with the darkness of vernacular architecture by combining white-rendered brick in the lower part of the facades with dark-stained wood cladding in the upper parts of the volume.

The site engineer's house, which later functioned as a company guesthouse, has a slightly fan-shaped plan. The pitched roof folds softly to an almost concave form on the rear of the house, one of Aalto's free-form rooflines that he favored during the 1950s. The main entrance is reached from the side, with the living room opening at a ninety-degree angle, another familiar element of Aalto's houses. The main rooms form a diagonal sequence of almost one unified space, as the openings between the rooms are wide. Facing westward, they are oriented toward the afternoon and evening sunlight. The private bedrooms, on the ground floor, open directly onto a small private courtyard.

Top and bottom
**Views of the semi-detached
houses from the street**

In the design for the site manager's house, Aalto repeated the room arrangement and general volume of the site engineer's house, but refined them spatially and architecturally. The house fully exploits the slope of the site with two one-story wings that serve different functions: the public rooms are in the upper wing, while the private home is on the lower level, with the kitchen and service facilities uniting the two. This kind of arrangement ensured that entertaining guests wouldn't disturb the family life, and vice versa. The private wing contains a separate family living room and a spacious hall with a fireplace, which connects to a small yard.

The upper floor has a fan-shaped plan, with a library, living room, and dining room facing west to catch the evening sun and opening onto a terraced garden. The inner landscape culminates in the living room where the irregular rhythm of the gently stepped wooden ceiling is reminiscent of a hilly landscape and accompanies the roof's wave-shaped ridge form. The room sequence is characterized by an airiness and elegance of proportions.

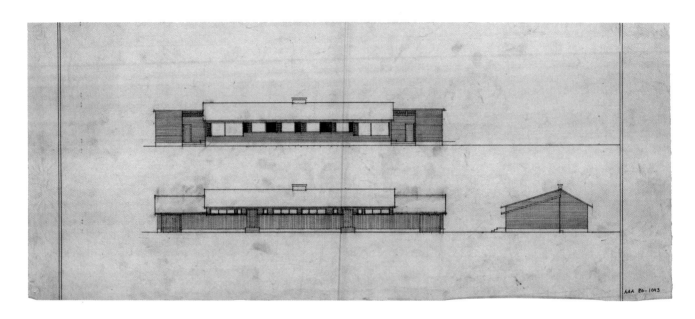

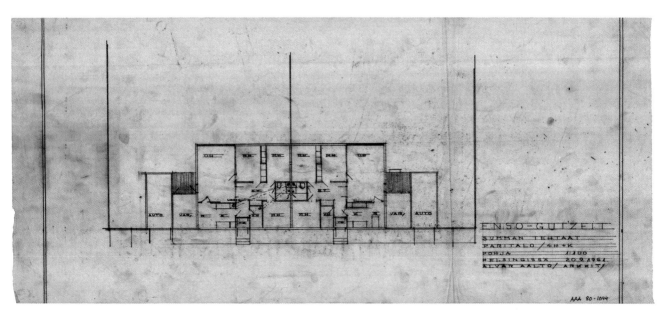

opposite top
**Semi-detached houses,
facade drawings**

opposite bottom
**Semi-detached houses,
floor plan**

below
Living room

top
**Engineers' houses, north
and south facades**

bottom
Engineers' houses, site plan

opposite
**Site engineer's house,
south facade**

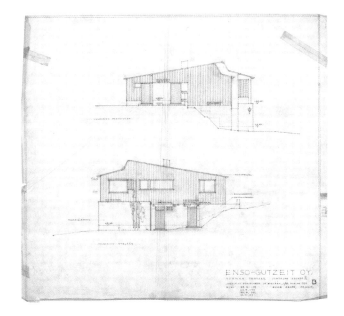

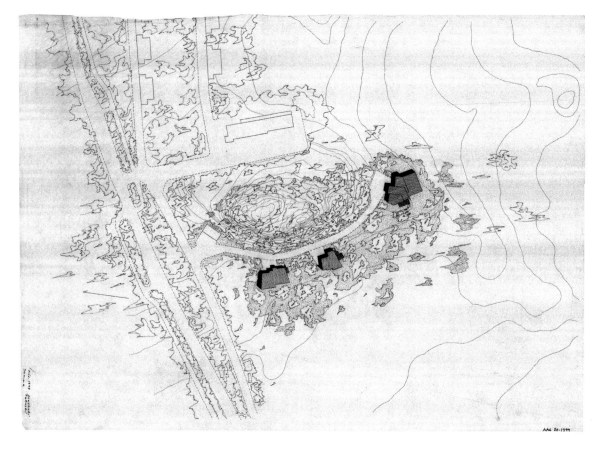

top
The site engineer's
house merges with its
surroundings.

bottom
View of the house from
the east

top
The fireplace corner is a central part of the living room.

bottom
View of the living room and the green forest beyond

top
Main entrance

middle
Plan sketches

bottom
West facade

opposite
The winter evening lights reveal the inner landscape of the living room with its stepped ceiling.

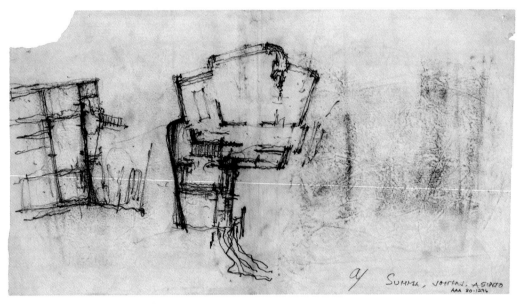

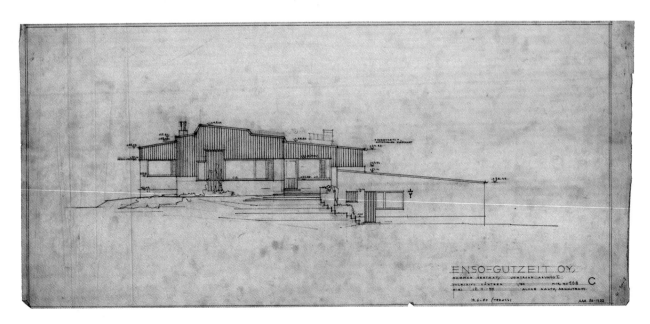

below
Living room

opposite
**The interplay of the
fan-shaped space,
the rhythm of the windows,
and the stepped form of
the ceiling characterizes
the living room.**

The 1960s: Houses for Friends

During the 1960s Finland became increasingly industrialized, and small-scale agriculture began to decline, with the result that rural areas became depopulated, while urban communities were growing. Finland's welfare structures were strengthened, and the standard of living rose. There was liberation and internationalization in the air. In the building and construction industry, prefabrication and standardization played an important role.

For Aalto's office the 1960s meant many foreign projects and public buildings in Finland, such as the Finlandia Hall in Helsinki (1962–71, 1975) and the administrative and cultural centers in Jyväskylä (1964–70 and 1977–82) and Seinäjoki (1957–87). Aalto's position among his colleagues was ambiguous during this decade. On the one hand, he was respected for his life's work and his official status as a member of the Finnish Academy. On the other hand, a younger generation of architects began to look at the world through a very different lens. Interested in global issues, universal systems and structures, and geometric simplicity in the spirit of Mies van der Rohe, they considered Aalto's buildings too individual and even elitist. His architecture certainly became more monumental and was often expressed in luxurious materials, such as marble. In the daily office routine his role had become that of the maestro, while the practical work on the drawing board and on building sites was mostly left to office staff. The houses Aalto designed during this decade were all commissioned by friends, and their personalities and interests are clearly present in the buildings.

opposite
**Villa Kokkonen,
detail of the living
room fireplace**

Maison Aho

Rovaniemi, Finland
1964–65

The first house Aalto designed in the 1960s was a residence for Aarne and Hilda Aho in the Finnish town of Rovaniemi. The architect had a long history with Rovaniemi, which had started in the mid-1940s, when he drew, in collaboration with architects Yrjö Lindegren (1900–1952) and Viljo Rewell (1910–1964), a new master plan, the so-called Reindeer Antler Plan, for the destroyed town.[1] In the latter half of the 1950s he also designed the garden city–like residential area Korkalonrinne there and was commissioned by local businessman and commercial councilor Aarne Aho to design three business and apartment houses in the center of the town.[2] Aho had been a member of the administrative committee steering the Rovaniemi reconstruction and had known Aalto since the mid-1940s.[3] In 1964, when the architect was working on yet another Rovaniemi project, the library, Aho's wife, Hilda Aho, wrote to ask if he would design a small two-family house for the couple.[4] The Maison Aho was completed the following year.

Located on a verdant residential block in the center of Rovaniemi, the house is introverted at first sight. The entranceway from the street is quietly hidden behind a red brick wall, which demarcates the garden from the neighboring plots and park area. Only one window overlooks the street. Like many other Aalto houses Maison Aho turns its back to the street and faces the garden. Due to the slightly sloping site the house has only one floor on the street side and two on the garden side, further emphasizing the contrast between enclosure and opening.

The Aho family had a large art collection they wanted to showcase in the house, and the Maison Carré became a natural model. Immediately upon entering, visitors encounter a longitudinal, slightly curving gallery wall that dominates the hall space, which seamlessly flows into the spacious living room. The hall functions as an intermediate space with an ambiguous character. While it serves as a gallery, it is also an integral part of the living room and links the formal rooms of the house together. The importance of spatial movement is emphasized with three wide steps that lead from the entrance hall into the living room and gallery space. These few steps also give the hall a public ambience that is further accentuated by the skylight above the gallery wall, which provides indirect natural light to illuminate the artwork. Concealed behind the gallery wall is a narrow corridor leading to the master bedroom, the kitchen, and other private rooms. This separation of everyday spaces from those with a more public role follows the same principle Aalto used in several other private houses.

The plan is slightly fan-shaped, with the gallery hall functioning as a hinge; its space narrows toward

the dining room end, while the fan opens in the living room. A large corner window in the living room faces west to capture the afternoon sunlight, illuminating a display of sculptures on the broad window sills. The high quality of materials and craftsmanship throughout the house underlines the refinement of the interior. A corner column and the fireplace in the living room have marble finishing, a material, which for Aalto was a symbol of classical architecture, and which he favored especially during his late years.

The elegance of materials is evident on the exterior as well. Warm red brick walls are complemented by copper details and roofing, while the plinths are veiled by black granite. This material palette was typical for Aalto who used it since the 1950s; one of his great passions was the quality of brickwork, evident in the Maison Aho's facades. In spite of this he originally intended the house to have a light-colored exterior—either through rendering or the use of specially made light brick—but due to the clients' distrust in the durability of the surface in the northern climate, the final choice was red brick.[5] Small terraces tie the house to the garden, which features several pine trees whose colors interact with the red brick.

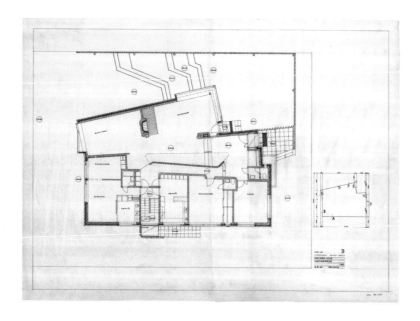

opposite top
Floor plan

opposite bottom
Northeast facade

top
The house's main entrance from the northwest is hidden behind a brick wall.

bottom
A view of the house from the neighboring park

opposite

The hall with the gallery
wall flows into the living room.
Designed for Aarne Aho's
collection of Finnish art,
the gallery wall and skylight
are the most important
elements of the house.

bottom

The living room features
a broad panoramic window
and a corner column clad
with marble strips. On
the window sill are sculptures
by Kari Huhtamo, Kalervo
Kallio, and Heikki Häiväoja.
The chandelier is made of
Murano glass.

top

The skylight in the hall
illuminates the artworks
with indirect natural light.
The wooden statue in the
background is by Johannes
Haapsalo (1920).

The entrance hall welcomes visitors with paintings by Christina Snellman from the 1960s (the large ones) and the 1980s (the small ones). The steel sculpture on the right is Kari Huhtamo's *Steel Construction* (1973) and the bronze rooster is by Helvi Hyvärinen (1950s).

Kitchen. The blue and white pendant lamp, type number A335, was designed in 1955 and the "L"-leg chairs are from 1934–36.

Marble accents the living room fireplace. On the right are three paintings by the Lappish artist Reidar Särestöniemi. *Poro (The Reindeer)* is from 1963, the blue landscape from 1962, and the female figure is from the 1950s. The sculptures on the fireplace are by Wäinö Aaltonen (1894–1966), the most important Finnish sculptor during the late 1920s to 1950s.

Villa Oksala

Korpilahti, Finland
1965–66, 1974

Professor Päivö Oksala, a Latinist, scholar of antiquity, and professor of classical languages at Jyväskylä University, was a close and long-time friend of Aalto's. He played a seminal role in many of the town's cultural activities and actively promoted Aalto in Jyväskylä, eventually initiating the founding of the Alvar Aalto Museum in 1966.

The Oksala family owned an island with rocky, barren terrain in Lake Päijänne and decided to build a small summer cottage there. On a visit to the island with the Oksalas and Elissa in 1964, Aalto chose a site for the building, adjacent to a low cliff and with a view of the lake. From the very beginning he had a non-rectangular plan shape in mind for the small cabin. He sketched for a while sitting on the cliff and even suggested a bar-cum-kitchen.[6] The final version of the cottage was drawn in 1974 when it was also built.

The Villa Oksala is rooted between the rocks and trees of the island landscape, its fan shape sitting firmly beside a sheltering low mound of bedrock. Its natural stone plinth, for which boulders were collected from the lake shoreline, and gray wooden walls blend with the surroundings.

The compact volume of the cottage takes advantage of its fan shape. On the narrow end are the small entrance space, bedrooms, and kitchen, while the living room widens and opens a view to the lake through panoramic windows. As the height of the room increases as well—the ceiling following the angle of the roof—the room seems to be larger than it is. The use of natural materials continues inside; the interior walls and ceiling are clad with red pine boarding and the fireplace at the heart of the cabin is made of red brick. A small corner in the living room was separated with bookshelves to form a study for Päivö Oksala. Today furniture and lamps by Aalto are an inseparable part of the interior.

opposite
Seen from the lake, the Villa Oksala blends into the rocks and trees of the island.

top
Site plan

middle
Floor plan

bottom
**Drawings of the
Oksala sauna**

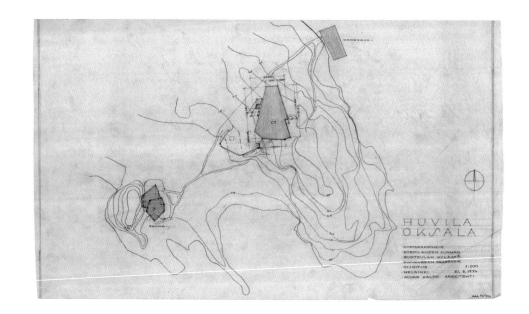

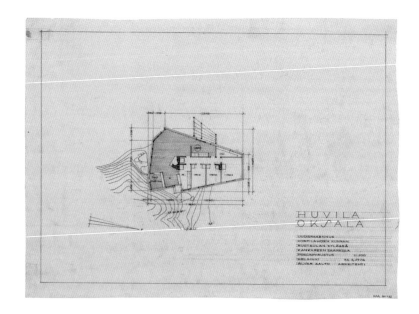

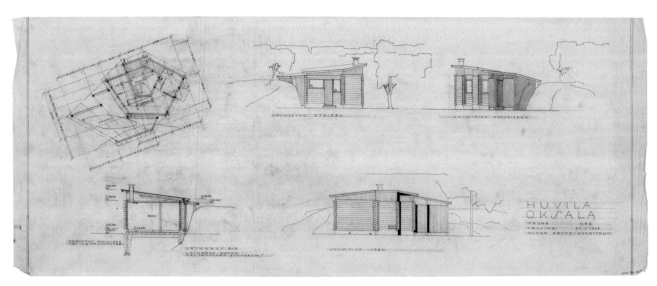

top
The fan-shaped sauna is reminiscent of Aalto's own smoke sauna at the Muuratsalo Experimental House.

bottom
South elevation

left
This view of the living room shows the work area in the corner. The armchair group in the center was designed in an earlier version for the Villa Mairea in 1938–39.

Villa Kokkonen

Järvenpää, Finland
1967–69

Composer Joonas Kokkonen (1921–1996) and Alvar Aalto first met in the 1950s, but became friends during the following decade when they were both members of the Finnish Academy. Work on the Villa Kokkonen began in 1963, when the composer called Aalto to ask whether one of the architect's assistants could design a house for him. Aalto's response was that while he did not design private houses any longer, he would make an exception for Kokkonen—and it would not be the work of an assistant. The first sketches for the house were drawn on a restaurant tablecloth after Aalto's first visit to the site, a location in Järvenpää near Lake Tuusulanjärvi. The architect started the sketch by drawing a grand piano, around which the plan of the house took shape, emphasizing the important role music would play in the design of the building. The first large musical work that Kokkonen composed in the Villa Kokkonen was a cello concerto that he dedicated to Aalto.[7]

The house turns its back to the street with a facade of dark-stained wooden battens, whose enclosed character is only interrupted by the atelier and living room fenestration. The main entrance canopy with its large sculptural form is an exception-ally dramatic element among Aalto houses, whose entrances are often modest and without any accents. The free-form treatment of the Villa Kokkonen's canopy resembles the silhouette of a hill landscape, a motif that emerged in Aalto's 1950s and 1960s

houses in various versions and contexts, such as roof shapes, sections of interior spaces, or forms of fireplaces.

The composition of the house is based on a fan shape, which is divided into three units, one housing the private rooms, kitchen, and auxiliary rooms; the middle area comprising the dining room and the living room; and the third part taken up by the atelier, which is separated acoustically from the rest of the house both through its placement and a soundproof sliding door.

Work is at the center of the house. The atelier wing, which is by far the largest space, dominates the volume with its height and shape. Its warm wooden interior surfaces were partly chosen for their acoustic qualities and contrast with the dark exterior. The atelier is like a musical box and was intended not only for composing but also for intimate chamber-music concerts. The space is divided into two parts, according to use; the grand piano clearly dominates the enclosed darker end of the room, while the other side with high windows facing southwest features a sofa corner and an imposing fireplace. Structural beams are exposed in the ceiling, partly concealed by a bellied fabric, which serves an acoustic purpose but also defines the area of the sofa corner. The fireplaces both in the atelier and adjacent living room take the sculptural element of the roof canopy inside in their free-form shapes. A skylight provides natural

opposite
Garden facade

light to the dining room. Here Aalto also used one of his favorite themes, hanging electric lamps from the skylight as a continuation of daylight.

Like in the Villa Mairea, a separate sauna, connected to the house by a pergola, is located at the far end of the plot. Its log structure is reminiscent of traditional Finnish countryside saunas and log cabins. The garden has two distinct areas: next to the atelier is a spruce forest with a dark and gloomy atmosphere, while the view from the living room opens onto a terraced lawn with lush shrubs and vines.

Villa Kokkonen is presently owned by the city of Järvenpää and operated as a museum. The building also serves as a venue for meetings and live music performances.

top
West facade

bottom left
First-floor plan

bottom right
From left to right: Alvar Aalto, Maija Kokkonen, Joonas Kokkonen, and Elissa Aalto in the garden of the Villa Kokkonen, ca. 1969

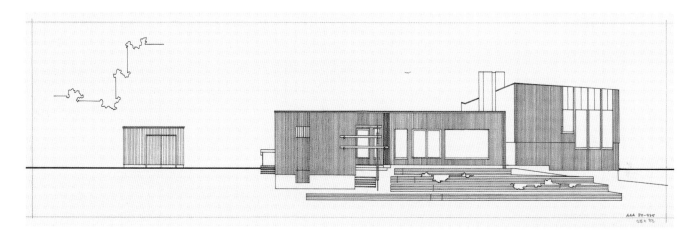

top
**Garden facade with the
atelier on the right, the living
room in the middle, and an
arbor pergola leading to the
sauna on the left**

bottom
**Entrance facade facing
eastwards to the street**

opposite
Joonas Kokkonen in his studio in 1996. The canvas stretched across the ceiling was applied to achieve better acoustics, but it also creates a kind of canopy for the sofa group. The bronze statue on the left, a bust of Joonas Kokkonen, is by Heikki Häiväoja (1991). On the floor is a wooden sculpture by Mauno Hartman, who also designed the stage set for Kokkonen's most well-known opera, *The Last Temptations* (1975).

below
Skylight and pendant lamps in the dining room. The lamps are an early 1960s variation of the Hand Grenade model.

below
**The grand piano in the
corner of the studio**

opposite
Living room

Villa Skeppet (Villa Schildt)

Tammisaari, Finland
1969–70

The last private house Aalto designed belonged to author and art historian Göran Schildt (1917–2009), who was a longtime friend of Aalto's. The two had met a few times in the 1940s but their friendship started in 1952, when Schildt arranged a meeting between Aalto and the Italian artist and designer Roberto Sambonet (1924–1995). The three men developed a close friendship during the following decade, and in the mid-1950s Aalto also designed a villa and studio for Sambonet, although it was never built.

Schildt's father had died when he was eight years old, and the architect would become a father figure to him.[8] Known as a travel writer and art critic, Schildt also was the author of several books on Aalto, the most extensive and notable being a three-volume biography of the architect, published between 1982 and 1989. From the mid-1960s on, Schildt and his wife Christine spent much of their time on the Greek island of Leros, where they had a vacation house. According to the writer, the project for the Villa Skeppet started with the following comment by Aalto: "You spend too much time abroad. I'll build you a house that makes you stay in Finland."[9] A passion for the Mediterranean united the two men, who were fascinated by its landscape, culture, and civilization. Aalto's most beloved country was Italy, while for Schildt Greece, and especially its archipelago, became a second home.

In Finland the Schildts came to live in the small coastal town of Tammisaari, where the Villa Skeppet is located on a quiet seaside street. *Skeppet*, meaning boat or vessel, refers to the appearance of the house, whose living room and balcony are like the commanding deck of a ship.[10] The villa's name could also symbolize Schildt's famous travels on his sailing boat *Daphne* in the Mediterranean Sea since the 1940s.

On the exterior the house is dominated by the living room corner, which rises up in the shape of a prow, and a wedge-shaped balcony that protrudes above the main entrance. This composition of angular and sharp forms has some kinship with the volumes of Finlandia Hall, designed around the same time. Inside, the villa is divided into four distinct parts, the most visible and complex being the large entrance hall/living room space. A separate small wing in the most peaceful and quiet corner of the house is reserved for Schildt's study. The kitchen area and bedroom are grouped together into a third unit, and a detached guestroom and sauna building is linked to the main house by a canopy and pergola. Behind the building is a pleasant garden, sheltered by a garden shed and wooden fence, with a small water-lily pond.

The spatial hierarchy is expressed both in the volume and exterior materials, with all facades made of white-rendered brick walls except that of

the living room and balcony, which are clad in dark-stained wood. White-painted wooden latticework is used as a visual shelter between the main house and the sauna building. The cantilevered balcony extends beyond the permitted building area for the foundations, a clever trick that allows for additional floor space and a better view for the living room.[11]

During the design and construction phases, Christine and Göran Schildt exchanged many letters with Aalto, discussing details and specific wishes of the couple, such as the colors for the bathroom and kitchen, or sizes and placements of windows and doors. One special dream of Schildt's was having a room furnished in an Ibsen-like style with late-nineteenth-century furniture, which was realized in the guest room.

The main staircase in the hall, defined by simple white brick walls, plays a central role in the spatial sequence of rooms and movement through the house. Describing the design process of the Villa Skeppet, Schildt wrote:

> I knew that Alvar was particularly attracted by steps. To him, they meant a meeting point between the human frame and the earth, an event where our legs measure the differences in levels of the terrain. Points of contact like this have been expressed at a larger scale in the cultivated terraces that people have been using since time immemorial to tame the wild forces of nature. Alvar loved these terraces in the mountain villages and hill towns of the Mediterranean countries. I did not think it would be possible to equip our Tammisaari house with this Aalto speciality. But what happened? When the house was eventually drawn up, I saw that despite the modest difference in levels Alvar had succeeded in squeezing in four steps in front of the main entrance door, five from the entrance hall to the first floor and courtyard level, and from there ten steps up to the large living room. So we were not left without this important stepping theme.[12]

Visitors get a first glimpse of the living room with its exposed ceiling beams from the ground floor entrance. Walking up the stairs, they experience the space gradually unfolding itself. On the mid-level they pass by a small hall with a view of the garden, and Schildt's study and the kitchen. The walls of the study are lined with books and the room breathes a cozy and cultivated atmosphere. Upstairs, the pointed and angled space of the living room is dynamic, with walls and a ceiling that have their own geometry. The wood-clad ceiling in particular is reminiscent of the interior of a sailing boat, a nod toward Schildt's lifelong love for the sea and sailing. Another strong element is the fireplace with its flame-shaped surface. A large corner window provides a view of the seashore park. The interior design is a combination of Aalto furniture and Mediterranean culture, with Greek amphorae next to the architect's glass vases.

Today the house is a private home.

VILLA SCHILDT

HUVUDPLAN 1/50 HELSINGFORS 23.10.1969 ALVAR AALTO

top
Göran Schildt in his study
in 1995. On the left is a
scale model of Schildt's sail
boat, *Daphne*.

bottom
Prototype of a Paimio chair
from 1932 next to a Greek
amphora. The untitled collage
on the door is by Mauno
Hartman (1978).

opposite
Staircase leading from the
entrance hall to the living
room. On the wall are Aalto's
laboratory experiments
with laminated wood (the
larger one from 1931 and
the smaller one from 1937).
In between is a pencil drawing
of Christine Schildt by Roberto
Sambonet (1984).

below
The flame-shaped fireplace
dominates the rear wall of the
living room. The blue painting
to its left, *Mediterranean Sea*
(1972), is by Sambonet.

top
Collection of Aalto vases
from 1936. The tall ones
are variations of the
Eskimoerindens skinnbuxa
(Eskimo Woman's Leather
Pants) series, from 1936.
The red and black Savoy vases
were originally designed by
Aino and Alvar Aalto for the
interior of the Savoy
Restaurant in Helsinki
(1936–37).

bottom
Dining room with the
half-open kitchen in the
background. The table cloth,
H-55, was designed by Elissa
Aalto in 1955. The pendant
lamp, type number A203, from
1953 was made for the
Säynätsalo Town Hall.

right
View of the living room with the stepped and elevated ceiling above the entrance area. On the left is an oil painting by Aalto, a gift to Göran Schildt. Aalto designed the pendant lamp in 1954. The tea trolley is from 1937 and was made for the Paris International Exhibition. The polyptych with four miniatures is by Sambonet (1955).

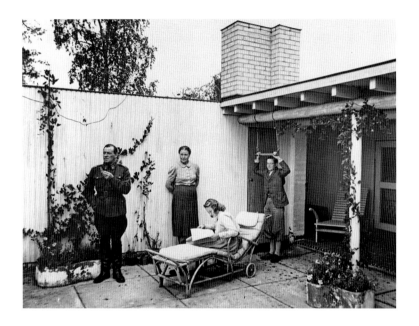

left
Alvar and Aino Aalto with their children, Heikki (Hamilkar) and Hanna-Maija (Hanni), on the Aalto House roof terrace during the Continuation War in 1941

right
The newlyweds Alvar and Elissa Aalto at the Muuratsalo Experimental House in the early 1950s

Biographies

Alvar Aalto

Born in Kuortane on February 3, 1898

1916 Matriculation from the Jyväskylä
Classical Lyceum

1921 Diploma in architecture from the Institute
of Technology, Helsinki

1923–27 Private architectural office in Jyväskylä
(in collaboration with Aino Aalto since 1924)

1924 Marriage to architect Aino Marsio (1894–1949)

1927–33 Private architectural office in Turku

1933–76 Private architectural office in Helsinki

1935 Founded Artek together with Aino Aalto,
Maire Gullichsen, and Nils-Gustav Hahl

1943–58 Chairman of the Association of Finnish
Architects (SAFA)

1946–48 Professor at the Massachusetts Institute
of Technology

1952 Marriage to architect Elsa Mäkiniemi

1955–68 Member of the Finnish Academy

1963–68 President of the Finnish Academy

1976 Died in Helsinki on May 11

Aino Marsio-Aalto

Born in Helsinki on January 25, 1894
née Aino Mandelin (from 1906 onwards Marsio)

1913 Matriculated from Helsingin Suomalainen
Tyttökoulu (Helsinki Finnish Girls' School)

1920 Diploma in Architecture, Institute of Technology,
Helsinki

1920 Started work in Oiva Kallio's office in Helsinki

1923 Worked in the office of Gunnar A. Wahlroos
in Jyväskylä

1924 Joined Alvar Aalto's office

1924 Marriage to Alvar Aalto

1935 Founded Artek together with Alvar Aalto,
Maire Gullichsen, and Nils-Gustav Hahl

1941 Became managing director of Artek

1949 Died in Helsinki, on January 13

Elissa Aalto

born in Kemi on November 22, 1922
née Elsa Kaisa Mäkiniemi

1941 Matriculated from Rovaniemen Yhteislyseo

1948 Diploma in Architecture, Institute of Technology,
Helsinki

1949 Started work in Alvar Aalto's office in Helsinki

1952 Marriage to Alvar Aalto

1994 Died in Helsinki, on April 12

Selected Works

Apartment building Aira for railway workers,
Jyväskylä, Finland, 1924–26

Jyväskylä Workers' Club, Jyväskylä, Finland, 1924–25

Seinäjoki Defence Corps Building, Seinäjoki,
Finland, 1924–26

Muurame Church, Muurame, Finland, 1926–29

Southwestern Finland Agricultural Cooperative
Building, Turku, Finland, 1927–28

Vyborg Library, Vyborg (now Russia), 1927, 1934–35

Paimio Tuberculosis Sanatorium, Paimio, Finland,
1929–33

Turun Sanomat Building, Turku, Finland, 1928–30

Toppila-Vaara pulp mill, Oulu, Finland, 1930–33

Savoy Restaurant interior, Helsinki, Finland, 1936–37

Sunila pulp mill and residential area, Kotka,
Finland, 1936–39, 1945–47, 1951–54

Finnish Pavilion at the Paris International Exhibition,
Paris, France, 1936–37 (demolished)

Inkeroinen master plan and housing, Kouvola,
Finland, 1937–1940s

Kauttua Factory and Housing, Eura, Finland,
1937–1940s

Finnish Pavilion at the New York World's Fair 1939,
New York, NY, USA, 1938–39 (demolished)

Senior Dormitory at the Massachusetts Institute of
Technology, also known as the Baker House,
Cambridge, MA, USA, 1946–49

Poetry Room at Harvard University, Cambridge,
MA, USA, 1948

Helsinki University of Technology, Otaniemi Campus,
Espoo, Finland, 1949–78

Säynätsalo Town Hall, Jyväskylä, Finland, 1949–52

Typpi company, factory and housing area, Oulu,
Finland, 1950–63

Rautatalo commercial building, Helsinki, Finland,
1951–55

Jyväskylä Institute of Pedagogics (Jyväskylä
University), Jyväskylä, Finland, 1951–71

Paper mill and housing in Summa, Hamina,
Vehkalahti, Finland, 1951–58

House of Culture, Helsinki, Finland, 1952–58

National Pensions Institute, Helsinki, Finland, 1948,
1953–57

Hansaviertel apartment building, Berlin, Germany,
1955–57

Studio Aalto at Munkkiniemi, Helsinki, Finland,
1954–55, 1962–63

Vuoksenniska Church and vicarage, Imatra, Finland,
1955–58

Finnish Pavilion in Venice's biennale park, Venice,
Italy, 1955–56

Seinäjoki administrative and cultural center,
Seinäjoki, Finland, 1951, 1958–87

Central Finland Museum, Jyväskylä, Finland,
1957–62

North Jutland Art Museum, Aalborg, Denmark, 1958,
1966–72

Neue Vahr apartment building, Bremen, Germany,
1958–62

Wolfsburg Cultural Center, Wolfsburg, Germany,
1958–62

Essen opera and music theater, Essen, Germany,
1959, 1983–88

Enso-Gutzeit company head offices, Helsinki,
    Finland, 1959–62
Wolfsburg Church, parish center, and vicarage,
    Wolfsburg, Germany, 1960–62
The Academic Bookstore, Helsinki, Finland, 1961,
    1966–69
Kaufman Rooms at the Institute of International
    Education, New York, NY, USA, 1961–65
Västmanlands-Dala Students Union building,
    Uppsala, Sweden, 1961–65
Rovaniemi administrative and cultural center,
    Rovaniemi, Finland, 1961–88
Finlandia Hall, Helsinki, Finland, 1962, 1967–71,
    1973–75
Nordic House, Reykjavik, Iceland, 1962, 1970–71
Schönbühl apartment building, Lucerne, Switzerland,
    1964–67
Library for Mount Angel Benedictine Abbey, St.
    Benedict, OR, USA, 1964, 1967–70
Riola Church, Riola, Italy, 1966, 1975–80, 1993–94
Lahti Church, Lahti, Finland, 1969–79
Alvar Aalto Museum, Jyväskylä, Finland, 1971–73

For more information on Alvar Aalto's works and
houses, see www.alvaraalto.fi.

Notes

Introduction

1 Göran Schildt, *Alvar Aalto: A Life's Work—Architecture, Design, and Art* (Helsinki: Otava Publishing Company, 1994).

2 Alvar Aalto, "From Doorstep to Living Room" (1926), in Göran Schildt, ed., *Alvar Aalto in His Own Words* (Helsinki: Otava Publishing Company, 1997).

3 Göran Schildt, *Alvar Aalto: The Early Years* (New York: Rizzoli International Publications, 1984), 254.

4 Aalto, "From Doorstep to Living Room," 50.

5 Ibid., 51.

6 Ibid., 51–52.

7 Le Corbusier, *Towards A New Architecture* (London: The Architectural Press and New York: Frederich A. Prager, 1959), 100.

8 Aalto, "From Doorstep to Living Room," 53.

9 Ibid., 55.

10 Ibid.

11 As quoted in Gary J. Coates, *Erik Asmussen, architect* (Stockholm: Byggförlaget, 1997), 230.

12 Alvar Aalto, "The Stockholm Exhibition, 1930" (1930), in Schildt, *Alvar Aalto in His Own Words*, 75–76.

13 Alvar Aalto, "The Dwelling as a Problem," in *Domus*, nos. 8–10 (1930). Reprinted in Schildt, *Alvar Aalto in His Own Words*, 77–78.

14 Ibid., 83.

15 Alvar Aalto, "Rationalism and Man" (1935), in Schildt, *Alvar Aalto in His Own Words*, 89–91.

16 Ibid., 93.

17 Aino and Alvar Aalto, "Villa Mairea: project description" (1939), in Juhani Pallasmaa, ed., *Alvar Aalto: Villa Mairea 1938–39* (Helsinki: Alvar Aalto Foundation and Mairea Foundation, 1998), 31.

18 Ibid.

19 Ibid.

20 Sigfried Giedion, *Space, Time and Architecture: The Growth of a New Tradition*, 2nd enlarged edition (Cambridge, Massachusetts: Harvard University Press, 1952), 490.

21 "Every decision is in some way a compromise, which can be attained most readily if we consider human beings at their weakest." Alvar Aalto, "Rationalism and Man," 92.

22 Interview of Alvar Aalto for Finnish Television, July 1972, in Schildt, *Alvar Aalto in His Own Words*, 274.

The 1920s

1 Göran Schildt, *Alvar Aalto: A Life's Work—Architecture, Design, and Art* (Helsinki: Otava Publishing Company, 1994), 207; Suomen rakennuskulttuurin yleisluettelo, Kohdeinventointilomake Jyväskylä [General Inventory of the Built Heritage in Finland, Jyväskylä], 1982.

2 Suomen rakennuskulttuurin yleisluettelo, Kohdeinventointilomake Laukaa [General Inventory of the Built Heritage in Finland, Laukaa], 1982.

3 Alvar Aalto, "From Doorstep to Living Room," in *The Early Years*, by Göran Schildt (New York: Rizzoli International Publications, 1984), 216.

4 Schildt, *Alvar Aalto: A Life's Work—Architecture, Design, and Art*, 178.

5 Aalto, "From Doorstep to Living Room," 216.

6 Mirjami Kaunismaa, "Mannerin talo," in *Töysän Joulu* ["The House of Manner," in *The Christmas of Töysä*] (Töysä: OAJ:n Töysän paikallisyhdistys [Töysä Local Association of Teachers' Union], 2004), 29–32.

7 Jari Jetsonen and Markku Lahti, *Alvar Aalto Houses* (Helsinki: Rakennustieto, 2005), 22.

8 Ibid., 33.

9 Aalto, "From Doorstep to Living Room," 215–16.

10 Kaunismaa, "Mannerin talo," 29–32.

11 Erkki Helamaa and Jari Jetsonen, *Alvar Aalto: Summer Homes* (Helsinki: Rakennustieto, 2007), 31.

12 Ibid., 34.

The 1930s

1 Göran Schildt, *Alvar Aalto: The Decisive Years* (Helsinki: Otava Publishing Company, 1986), 121–28, 139–44.

2 Olavi Granö, "On Finnish-Estonian Research Cooperation," in *Alvar Aalto—Villa Tammekann*, ed. Maija Mäkikalli and Henri Terho (Turku, Finland: The Turku University Foundation, 2000), 29–30.

3 August Tammekann to Alvar Aalto, 22 March 1932, Document Collection, Alvar Aalto Museum.

4 Irene Tammekann to Alvar Aalto, postcard, 22 June 1932, Document Collection, Alvar Aalto Museum.

5 Irene Tammekann to Alvar Aalto, 10 August 1932, Document Collection, Alvar Aalto Museum.

6 Paavo Tammekann, "The History of the Villa Tammekann," in *Alvar Aalto—Villa Tammekann*, ed. Mäkikalli and Terho, 130.

7 Alvar Aalto to the Tammekanns, n.d., Document Collection, Alvar Aalto Museum.

8 August Tammekann to Alvar Aalto, 4 November 1932, Document Collection, Alvar Aalto Museum.

9 Tammekann, "The History of the Villa Tammekann," 144; August Tammekann to Alvar Aalto, 21 January 1935, Document Collection, Alvar Aalto Museum.

10 Tapani Mustonen, "Villa Tammekann—A Living Construction Process," in *Alvar Aalto—Villa Tammekann*, ed. Mäkikalli and Terho, 200–203.

11 Renja Suominen-Kokkonen, "The Ideal Image of the Home," in *Alvar Aalto Architect*, vol. 6, *The Aalto House 1935–36*, ed. Juhani Pallasmaa (Helsinki: Alvar Aalto Academy, 2003), 14–15. Suominen-Kokkonen describes in detail the history and different phases of the Aalto House.

12 Ibid., 15–16.

13 Aino Aalto and Alvar Aalto, "The Aalto's Private House," in *Alvar Aalto Architect*, vol. 6, *The Aalto House 1935–36*, ed. Juhani Pallasmaa (Helsinki: Alvar Aalto Academy, 2003), 39.

14 Schildt, *Alvar Aalto: The Decisive Years*, 129–30. The Niemelä tenant farm with its several buildings dates from the eighteenth and nineteenth centuries and is part of the Seurasaari Open-Air Museum in Helsinki. The farm buildings are considered to present Finland's ancient tradition of log houses.

15 Pekka Korvenmaa, "Aalto and Finnish Industry," in *Alvar Aalto: Between Humanism and Materialism*, ed. Peter Reed (New York: Museum of Modern Art, 1998), 71–88.

16 Mia Hipeli, "Inkeroinen 1937–57," in *Alvar Aalto Architect*, vol. 7, *Sunila 1936–54*, ed. Pekka Korvenmaa (Helsinki: Alvar Aalto Academy, 2004), 132–38.

17 Korvenmaa, "Aalto and Finnish Industry," 79–80.

18 Juhani Pallasmaa, ed., *Alvar Aalto: Villa Mairea* (Helsinki: Alvar Aalto Foundation and Mairea Foundation, 1998), 31. Originally published as Aino Aalto and Alvar Aalto, "Mairea," *Arkkitehti*, no. 9 (1939): 134–137.

19 Schildt, *Alvar Aalto: The Decisive Years*, 156–60.

20 Pallasmaa, ed., *Alvar Aalto: Villa Mairea*, 31.

21 Eila Jokela, "Suuria töitä pienissä olosuhteissa," ["Great Works in Small Circumstances"] *Suomen Kuvalehti*, no. 34 (1958): 12, 38.

The 1940s

1 Göran Schildt, ed., *Alvar Aalto in His Own Words* (Helsinki: Otava Publishing Company, 1997), 153–54.

2 Pekka Korvenmaa, "Aalto and Finnish Industry," in *Alvar Aalto: Between Humanism and Materialism*, ed. Peter Reed (New York: Museum of Modern Art, 1998), 82–84.

3 *Tampereen rakennuskulttuuri, maisemat ja luonnonsuojelu* [The Built Heritage, Landscape and Natural Protection in Tampere, report] (Tampere, Finland: Tampere City Planning Office, 1985)

4 Ibid., 196.

5 Ibid.

6 "Miten asevelitaloissa asutaan?" ["How Do People Live in Ex-Servicemen Houses?"] in *Kotiliesi*, no. 19 (1943): 552–53, 574.

7 Göran Schildt, *Alvar Aalto: A Life's Work—Architecture, Design, and Art* (Helsinki: Otava Publishing Company, 1994), 188.

8 Maunu Häyrynen, ed., *Pihlavan Kaunismäki: Puutarhainventoinnin loppuraportti* [Kaunismäki in Pihlava: Report of the Garden Inventory] (Turku, Finland: Turku University, The Department of Cultural Production and Landscape Studies, 2005).

9 Lauri Putkonen and Marja Ivars, *Kyliä ja kortteleita: Hämeenlinnan ja Hattulan rakennuskulttuuriselvitys* [Villages and Quarters:

The Inventory of the Built Heritage in Hämeenlinna and Hattula] (Hämeenlinna, Finland: Hattulan kunta, Hämeenlinnan kaupunki, 2003), 112.

10 Erkki Helamaa and Jari Jetsonen, *Alvar Aalto: Summer Homes* (Helsinki: Rakennustieto, 2007), 46.

The 1950s

1 Alvar Aalto to the Helsinki Taxation Office, 5 July 1956, Document Collection, Alvar Aalto Museum.

2 Nils Erik Wickberg, "Alvar Aalto—A Full-length Portrait," in *Alvar Aalto 1998*, ed. Aila Kolehmainen, Esa Laaksonen, Leenamaija Laine, Maarit Seeling, and Katariina Séwon (Helsinki: the Finnish Association of Architects, 1999), 13. Nils Erik Wickberg, a long-time editor-in-chief of the Finnish architectural journal *Arkkitehti* and a professor at the Helsinki University of Technology, met Alvar and Aino Aalto in the late 1930s and was a family friend especially in the 1940s and 1950s.

3 Aalto's office to Jaakko Lehmus, 13 July 1955, Document Collection, Alvar Aalto Museum.

4 Alvar Aalto and Elissa Aalto, "La Maison Carré," in *Alvar Aalto Architect*, vol. 20, *Maison Louis Carré 1956–63*, ed. Esa Laaksonen and Ásdís Ólafsdóttir (Helsinki: Alvar Aalto Academy, 2008), 148.

5 Antoine Terrasse, "Louis Carré: A Life of Passion and Method," in *Alvar Aalto Architect*, vol. 20, *Maison Louis Carré 1956–63*, ed. Laaksonen and Ólafsdóttir, 125–27.

6 Esa Laaksonen, "'I Speak of What is Good,'" in *Alvar Aalto Architect*, vol. 20, *Maison Louis Carré 1956–63*, ed. Laaksonen and Ólafsdóttir, 8; Alvar Aalto, "To Will Grohmann," in *Alvar Aalto Architect*, vol. 20, *Maison Louis Carré 1956–63*, ed. Laaksonen and Ólafsdóttir, 181.

7 Irmelin Lebeer, "Interview with Louis Carré," in *Alvar Aalto Architect*, vol. 20, *Maison Louis Carré 1956–63*, ed. Laaksonen and Ólafsdóttir, 135–37.

8 Ásdís Ólafsdóttir, "A Home of Design and Art," in *Alvar Aalto Architect*, vol. 20, *Maison Louis Carré 1956–63*, ed. Laaksonen and Ólafsdóttir, 53.

9 Terrasse, "Louis Carré: A Life of Passion and Method," 127.

10 Pekka Korvenmaa, "Aalto and Finnish Industry," in *Alvar Aalto: Between Humanism and Materialism*, ed. Peter Reed (New York: Museum of Modern Art, 1998), 85.

The 1960s

1 Päivi Lukkarinen, *Aalto Lapissa: Alvar Aallon Lapin tuotanto* [Aalto in Lapland: Alvar Aalto's work in Lapland] (Jyväskylä, Finland: Atena Kustannus Oy, 1998), 33–40.

2 Ibid., 55–67.

3 Ibid., 75.

4 Ibid., 72–75; Hilda Aho to Alvar Aalto, 20 March 1964, Document Collection, Alvar Aalto Museum.

5 Lukkarinen, *Aalto Lapissa: Alvar Aallon Lapin tuotanto* [Aalto in Lapland: Alvar Aalto's work in Lapland], 75.

6 Louna Lahti, *Alvar Aalto—Ex intimo: Alvar Aalto through the Eyes of Family, Friends & Colleagues* (Helsinki: Building Information Ltd., 2001), 175.

7 Ibid., 65.

8 Göran Schildt, *Alvar Aalto: The Decisive Years* (Helsinki: Otava Publishing Company, 1986), 15; Lahti, *Alvar Aalto—Ex intimo*, 56–57.

9 Lahti, *Alvar Aalto—Ex intimo*, 55.

10 Göran Schildt to Alvar Aalto, 25 April 1971, Document Collection, Alvar Aalto Museum. Schildt describes how the townspeople have begun to call the house "skeppet."

11 Göran Schildt, "The Villa Skeppet—Its Design and Construction," in *Alvar Aalto: Villa Skeppet 1969–1970*, ed. Mia Hipeli, (Jyväskylä, Finland: Alvar Aalto Foundation, 2009), 21.

12 Ibid., 17.

Illustration Credits

All photographs © Jari Jetsonen unless otherwise noted. All drawings © Alvar Aalto Museum unless otherwise noted.

Page 10: Photo Italo Martinero, Alvar Aalto Museum
Page 11: Alvar Aalto Museum
Page 12 top: Freechristimages@live.com
Page 12 bottom: *Aitta* magazine (1926), page 65
Page 14 bottom: Alvar Aalto Museum
Page 15: Artek/Alvar Aalto Museum
Page 21: Masaaki Takahashi/Alvar Aalto Museum 1997
Page 54: Aalto family album/Alvar Aalto Museum, 1932
Page 63 top: Aalto family album/Alvar Aalto Museum, 1941
Page 63 middle right: Aalto family album/Alvar Aalto Museum, 1941
Page 73 top: Alvar Aalto Museum, 1937
Page 91 bottom: Alvar Aalto Museum, 1938
Page 107 top: Alvar Aalto Museum, 1943
Page 147 top: Alvar Aalto Museum
Page 162 bottom left: Alvar Aalto Museum, 1965
Page 162 bottom right: Photo Heikki Havas/Alvar Aalto Museum, 1959
Page 176 bottom: Masaaki Takahashi/Alvar Aalto Museum, 1997
Page 202 bottom right: Joonas Kokkonen family album/Alvar Aalto Museum, 1969
Page 210: Photo Mikko Merckling/Alvar Aalto Museum
Page 218 left: Photo Göran Schildt/Alvar Aalto Museum, 1950s
Page 218 right: Aalto family album/Alvar Aalto Museum, 1941

Published by
Princeton Architectural Press
37 East 7th Street, New York, NY 10003

For a free catalog of books, call 1-800-722-6657
Visit our website at www.papress.com

© 2011 Princeton Architectural Press, Jari Jetsonen, and Sirkkaliisa Jetsonen
All rights reserved
Printed and bound in China
14 13 12 11   4 3 2 1   First edition

Editor: Nicola Bednarek Brower
Designer: Paul Wagner

Special thanks to: Bree Anne Apperley, Sara Bader, Nicola Bednarek Brower, Janet Behning, Megan Carey, Carina Cha, Tom Cho, Penny (Yuen Pik) Chu, Russell Fernandez, Pete Fitzpatrick, Jan Haux, Linda Lee, John Myers, Katharine Myers, Dan Simon, Andrew Stepanian, Jennifer Thompson, Joseph Weston, and Deb Wood of Princeton Architectural Press —Kevin C. Lippert, publisher

Library of Congress Cataloging-in-Publication Data:
Jetsonen, Jari, 1958–
  Alvar Aalto houses / Jari Jetsonen and Sirkkaliisa Jetsonen ;
With an introduction by Juhani Pallasmaa. — 1st ed.
     p.   cm.
ISBN 978-1-56898-982-2 (alk. paper)
1. Aalto, Alvar, 1898-1976. 2. Architecture, Domestic—Finland—History—20th century. I. Jetsonen, Sirkkaliisa. II. Aalto, Alvar, 1898-1976. III. Title.
NA1455.F5A2435 2011
728'.37092—dc22
                                    2010029152